Texas Riverman

The Life and Times of Captain Andrew Smyth

Texas Riverman

The Life and Times of Captain Andrew Smyth

BY WILLIAM SEALE

University of Texas Press, Austin and London

For Kit

ACKNOWLEDGMENTS

Three people have played a major part in the construction of this book. My father, the late William Seale of Beaumont, Texas, preserved the steamer trunk and its contents; Professor Robert H. Woody, of Duke University, has advised me and given freely of his time; Mrs. George C. O'Brien, of Beaumont, has shared with me her recollections of the Jasper County which Andrew knew.

Mrs. Walter D. Brown of Beaumont has lent her editorial talents to the writing of the manuscript and has been a consultant on its construction.

Mr. and Mrs. Jack B. Osborne of Beaumont have been most helpful, both with the illustrations and with my use of legal details of Andrew's Texas.

My mother, Mrs. William Seale, has heard me read rough drafts, and has patiently criticized them; too, she has provided me with a quiet, pleasant place in which to work.

Mrs. Joe Myers, also of Beaumont, has willingly read documents and rough drafts of this manuscript.

I wish that I could list separately the contributions of the following people and institutions. All have been eager to help me, and they have my thanks: the late Mrs. John L. Appling, Mrs. George W. Armstrong, Mrs. Kurn Braswell, Mrs. W. J. Bridges, Mr. George P. Burris, Mr. John B. Cheesman, Mr. J. M. Childers, Mr. Richard Arlen Durdin, Mrs. Arthur Few, Mrs. Joe J. Fisher, Professor Earl W. Fornell, Mr. Arden Hooks, Mrs. Mary Seale Horn, Mr. Jack Josey, Mrs. Henry Koster, Mrs. Charles Martin, Miss Erin O'Brien, Mrs. Joe Owens, Judge and Mrs. James Parker, Mrs. Judith Powell, Mrs. Robert Roy, Miss Mattie Russell, Mr. Tom Sawyer, Mrs. Tom Schofield, Mrs. Curtis Franklin Scott, Mrs. Geraldine Goodhue, Mrs. James A. Talley, Mrs. John Walker, Mr. W. J. Wong, the University of Texas Library, the Texas State Archives, the University of North Carolina Library, the Library of Congress, the Alabama State Library, the Lamar State College Library, the Rosenberg Library, Mrs. Carmen Whatley of the Terrell Public Library, the University of Houston Library, and Mr. and Mrs. Smyth Walden and Mr. Smyth Walden, Jr., for Smyth materials in their collection.

INTRODUCTION

The Steamer Trunk

The biography of Andrew Smyth is the documented story of an obscure Texas riverman. Smyth's world is gone, and so few physical traces remain from his era that indeed he would not recognize his own locality. His story has been preserved in a little wooden steamer trunk, literally stuffed with letters from people he knew; in the trunk's fifty years of adventures from trash heap to attic no damage was done to the manuscripts. Even a cursory examination of the letters made the biography irresistible to write.

I

After her husband's funeral in Beaumont, Texas, in 1879 Mrs. Andrew F. Smyth made hasty arrangements for the future of his business enterprises, altering as little as possible. The steamer *Laura*, his main investment, needed a new captain; Mrs. Smyth's standing in relation to the other investors had to be established on paper. When everything had been attended to she boarded the *Laura* for the family home at Bevilport, seventy miles upriver.

On the trip Mrs. Smyth went through the papers in Captain Smyth's office and evidently decided to keep anything not necessary for the company records. For most of the twenty days' duration of the trip she stayed in the office, folding and packing, pausing now and then to read a letter or to remember the somber face in an old daguerreotype, which had been forgotten in a pigeonhole for years. Perhaps the Captain had aged toward the last. She had noticed it, and it was certainly apparent in the way in which he hoarded odd items. His papers, mostly letters and account books, were placed neatly in an old-fashioned steamer trunk, one she recalled that he had used for the thirty-five years he had spent on the river.

By the time the *Laura* reached Bevilport the office had lost its cluttered look and the steamer trunk could hold no more. In fact, it was remarkable that the top would close. Mrs. Smyth and her Negro servant, Ann-Tobe, worked their way through the well-meaning crowd at the Bevilport landing to a waiting spring wagon; then with their baggage and the steamer trunk they drove home.

In the house near Bevilport, Mrs. Smyth put the trunk in an obscure corner and forgot it, except for the rare occasions when she deposited or removed letters.

From neglect the steamer trunk's leather covering peeled and cracked, its brass studs tarnishing until they could not be distinguished from the rusty iron bands which held the trunk together. A granddaughter finally made a cotton skirt to hide its unsightliness.

Years passed, and the world through which the Captain had carried his steamer trunk became very different. Steamboats disappeared from the rivers. The *Laura* sank to the bottom of the Neches in the port of Beaumont, leaving her stack poking above the surface of the water some three feet, as if to please the birds who roosted there. Bevilport, the river town, rotted, and then was gone, except for a brick chimney which had once warmed the dining room of the hotel. Trees and brambles filled what had been cotton fields, even in sight of the Smyth house.

Mrs. Smyth, from her porch, could see changes, both in her thinning orchards and in the silence of the countryside. She made little effort to maintain the farm as the Captain had kept it. Fences fell and the best furniture was divided among the married children. Two of her children lived with her and managed the property which the Captain had left. Only when her grandchildren came to visit did things seem really alive again. But through the years she stayed there, sometimes under a sun-bonnet in her vegetable garden, other times too tired to do anything but sew.

Mrs. Smyth died in the winter of 1907. The homeplace was occupied by a member of the family until the early 1920's, at which time a new tenant emptied it of the captain's furniture and refurnished it with brass beds and golden oak. Other kinsmen were invited to come and take what they wanted of the old things.

Andrew Smyth's steamer trunk seems to have been an undesirable item, because it soon ended up sixty miles away in a dirt-floored wood-shed, barely protected from the rain. In 1945 it was given to my father, the late William Seale, a grandson of Captain Smyth, who stored it in the attic of his office in Beaumont.

II

This book, based for the most part on the contents of the steamer trunk, began as a Master of Arts thesis at Duke University and has been revised

TEXAS IN THE 1800's

for publication. The papers themselves have determined the flow of the story. In the book I have tried to recreate in fast narrative form the Texas and the way of life the Captain knew. I have had to rearrange fences and imagine ruined buildings as they might once have been. But most of all there is Andrew Smyth, whose name in official documents never appears outside an occasional land lease in one of several East Texas courthouses, and in a muster roll or two buried in a great public archive. He was a plain countryman, but one who delighted in the days he lived.

Getting to know Andrew Smyth has been a pleasant experience; putting his life into a book has merely been my way of transmitting that experience. This is the story of what happened to one man among the nameless thousands who migrated to Texas in the 1830's, eager to create, if not to find, a promised land.

William Seale
Smyth Homestead
Jasper County
Texas

CONTENTS

LIST OF ILLUSTRATIONS

(following page 66)

PART ONE

The Western Woods

1. Andrew Farney Smyth, seated beside a window in the chilly living quarters of his father's gristmill, tried again to start a letter to his brother. He had always found it the most difficult of tasks to express himself in writing, and the difficulty showed in his letters. The faculty of the local Presbyterian academy once observed that had Andrew's ability with words been half what it was in arithmetic, he would be among the best students in school. With arithmetic he was at home, because he felt that it would be useful someday and because it was akin to his slow, methodical way of thinking. Words were not as dependable: set down to say one thing, they came out with an entirely different meaning, or so it seemed to Andrew.

I

Now, if just for this particular day, he wanted to be able to write well for the brother, fourteen years his senior, whose own letters reflected the attitudes and polish of an educated man. In his mind Andrew worded and reworded sentences, adding all the phrases he could think of that might lend a sophisticated flavor to what he wanted to say.

Perhaps the drone of the millwheel outside arrested his thoughts and took them through many Aprils before this one, back to the memorable occasions of his seventeen years.

The best times seemed usually to come with the spring. April had never failed to bring the rise in Big Nance Creek, putting the mill into operation and thereby bringing money. Andrew had never been around much money, but all the Smyth children felt rich indeed in the spring, when their parents took them to town and bought them something which they had spent the summer, fall, and winter wanting very much. Even if hard work at the mill had been expected of the whole family during the spring rise, there had been a new rifle or a pony to think about, making the days and strenuous nights light spirited, pleasant. In the past few years Andrew's spring purchases had been small, because he had been a student at the academy, paying tuition. His younger brothers and sisters also would have the advantage of an education, although luxuries like new rifles and bonnets might necessarily be sacrificed to that end. On this particular day, at the peak of the spring rise, Andrew must have felt strange writing a letter instead of working at the mill with the rest of the family. During busy times none of the children went to school, but remained at home, at work. The reason why Andrew sat by himself in the low, log room was the letter which he did not know how to begin.

His father had instructed him to write his brother George and elaborate on the details of his mother's death four months before. The letter was to tell of her last seven nights' suffering, of her talk to the family when she had spoken of her readiness to meet God, and of their tears when she said it. The old miller knew that his eldest son, gone from home for five years, wanted to know all these particulars. On the day of her death Andrew's father put a note in the mail for George, but he had found himself unable to write more than a paragraph or two. George had written, asking to know more. Andrew was assigned to the task so that the father could return to his business. The presence of work to be done was good for a family that had lost one so close.

Scattered before Andrew on the table were pen, ink, and paper, and a lock of his mother's hair, tied with a black ribbon. The children had all been given locks of hair as remembrances.

To make his job easier, Andrew began the letter on one of the printed pages which his father had ordered at the newspaper office for distribution in the locality. A central block of black print, decorated on the sides with mourning designs, announced the death of Mrs. Susannah Smyth, and praised her nearness to the Presbyterian church and the "interesting children" that she left behind. Andrew had scrawled "Moulton, Alabama, April 12, 1835" at the top of the page when he first started to write. Now he formed the body of the letter.

The sentences came too quickly at first, each one in its blunt statement of fact revealing the writer's determination not to show emotions which he considered unmanly. Those bare descriptions, however, hid very little. Read thoughtfully, they were a tribute to the strong part which Susannah Smyth had played in the happiness of her plain household.

In the years when her husband had dreamed of a genteel life and had driven his family hard toward the goal of wealth which would have made it possible, it was Susannah who made the children anticipate real times, like spring, when especially good things, however small, could really happen. As constant as the creek rise, had been the miller's talk of moving to a new, richer part of the country, while his wife worked in the church, gathered her vegetables, and showed her sons and daughters that the good life could be found even on twenty of the sandiest, rockiest acres in Alabama. Those whose lives she had touched missed her.

A loneliness reflected in the letter of Andrew F. Smyth. The oldest by six years of the children at home, Andrew realized that life there was different now and, of necessity, would change more.

After he had related the sad account Andrew relaxed somewhat in his choice of words and rambled about happenings in town and about people that his brother probably remembered. Then he wrote of himself.

Finished with his course of study at the academy, he had met with difficulty in finding work. Now that his mother was gone it was more important than ever for him to leave the mill and gain employment elsewhere. Toward the end of the letter he wrote, "i wood receive a few lines from you with great pleasure i should like you to tell me what would be the prospect for a youth to make a living in that part of the country for it is but a slim chance here."

Finally folding the paper into a package, he inserted the lock of hair, and sealed the letter with red wax. The envelope was addressed to "George Washington Smyth, Texas, In the Western Woods."[1]

II

Andrew could not remember ever having been beyond the northern Alabama section in which he had grown up. He had lived here always, it seemed, in the mill with his parents at the foot of Little Mountain, halfway between the town of Moulton and the rocky shoals of the Tennessee River.

If not really certain where he had been born, he knew that the event had occurred in 1817 in a covered wagon on a Tennessee road. At that time his parents were on their way to Alabama, anxious to join Uncle Farney Smyth, who had settled near Moulton and had grown rich. The move to Moulton was not so rewarding for the rest of the Smyths. Uncle Farney, always restless and never dependable, had been unable to endure the recent death of his wife and had sold his land and Negroes some weeks before the appearance of his brother and sister-in-law. From the banks of the Tennessee River, Andrew's family watched him row out of sight, giving no explanation to the dejected figures on the shore, nor so much as a trinket for his infant namesake to remember him by. The baby had been called Farney until that time, as a token of appreciation for the uncle's invitation to come to Alabama; after the riverbank scene he was called Andrew, for his father.

[1] Andrew F. Smyth, Moulton, Alabama, to George W. Smyth, April 12, 1835. AFS MSS.

In this new place the parents, Andrew and Susannah, had been left to make something of themselves. Hard luck for them was nothing new; in the early years of the nineteenth century they had traveled from Pennsylvania to North Carolina, and then to Tennessee. They had burnt bridges with each move, confident that in the next place they would find success, and, maybe, as an afterthought, permanence. To have been greeted in Moulton, Alabama, by disappointment was discouraging, but there was nothing to do but remain and make the best of it.

During the years since then the Smyths had enjoyed simple comforts. Their house was a part of the mill, and the log edifice, perched on the bank of Big Nance Creek, had a pleasing look in its setting of pine, oak, and willow trees and the few flowers which Susannah had tended beside the door. The land behind the mill grew vegetables and was enclosed in part to house a community of chickens, ducks, horses, and hogs. While the mother's chief interest away from home was the church, the father kept informed on politics, which information gained for him the reputation of being an authority and the respectful title of Captain Smyth in the neighborhood.

Late in the 1820's the eldest son, George, had left home to return to Tennessee, where he had worked his way through school. Andrew and the younger children remained with their parents, enjoying the country pastimes of camp meetings, fairs in town, and weddings and funerals.

Shortly before his eighteenth birthday, in 1835, Andrew finished his courses at the academy; and when he had nothing to do at the mill he made short trips into nearby Moulton and Courtland to look for a job. The death of his mother increased his need of work because Captain Smyth had no place for him at home. In this coldest winter and spring which he had ever known, Andrew examined the various channels that might provide work. He wanted to get out on his own, to a place where he might realize high ambitions.

Captain Smyth depended upon him while he was at home but Andrew knew that he was a financial burden on his father. Being the eldest boy in the family after George left, Andrew had assumed the duties of a man when he was still very young. The Captain, possessed of a quick temper, would not tolerate foolishness in those he counted upon and could control. Consequently, Andrew had learned right away to take work seriously. His father had treated him as an adult, listening to his conversation understandingly and telling him of the great things that lay ahead for one who was not lazy.

Over the years, certain people in that part of the country had become rich and had built fine barns and houses. The Saunderses, close friends of the Captain, were in 1835 speaking of converting their Greek-revival mansion into a castle with battlements reminiscent of medieval romances. Had Captain Smyth been rich, that sort of thing was probably what he would have done.

There had been a time, Andrew knew, when dreams more than wealth characterized the region. The Smyths had dreamed then, but they dreamed now, too. People like the personable Saunderses had passed them up. Into the lives of the Smyths had been drawn basic comforts and the refinement of education, which they believed was a necessity on any economic level. Never had there been a ready supply of money, though, and rarely was there the cash with which to buy little luxuries from the stores of Moulton. Andrew longed to be rich, to have more than just a living. Indeed, his father made so little that to have an extra hand, at room and board alone, was a drain.

Timid in social endeavors, Andrew showed no reluctance to work, regardless of the job or the labor that might be involved. This business of making money was a grave matter to him, and eighteen was not too early an age to begin the climb toward what he wanted.

Andrew's investigation in the past weeks made it apparent that few of his ambitions could be satisfied even in the major towns of northern Alabama. In truth, Moulton and her sister cities offered faint savor to the appetite of a daydreaming youth. Moulton was a little village, the muddy streets of which were faced by a monotony of wooden buildings. The stage line had lately decided to stop a coach there regularly and that news, together with the public interest in the proposed brick courthouse, brought the only excitement that the town had known in a long time.[2] While Andrew's teachers had flattered his ability to comprehend arithmetic, the prospect of being a clerk in a settled place like this, even had the opportunity presented itself, was dreary. All the high pine-covered hills were claimed and used these many years; almost everything, from the thick vines on the porches to the smooth hide bottoms of the chairs, gave the district a complacent look. Had there been no alteration in his family's way of life, he might have shown reluctance at leaving.

But things had changed. To better himself at all, he was convinced that he would have to move on. Andrew's wish to go to a new place was undoubtedly influenced by the adventures of his oldest brother, whom he had last seen in the winter of 1830. Riding from Tennessee, George had

[2] *Ibid.*

that winter stopped by Big Nance Creek to tell his parents that he was headed for Texas in hopes of making his fortune. Andrew remembered the loud protests of his parents: the Captain knew the hardships of new land, and had good reason to object to George's plan; Susannah hated for her son to go so far away, and, Protestant that she was, was surely concerned by the fact that anyone entering that country had to declare himself a Roman Catholic. Still determined to go, George rode on, accepting reluctant blessings.[3]

Since that day, five years before, every footfall on the road or bark of the dogs sent Captain Smyth and Susannah hurrying to the door, certain that George had come to his senses and returned home.[4] But George did not return and the flow of his optimistic letters from Texas to Moulton evidenced that he liked what he had found.

Certainly, the letters from Texas held a great fascination for the whole Smyth family, not least of all young Andrew. The Smyths, like most Americans, knew vaguely the Texas story.

Mexico had declared her independence from Spain in 1821 and in that year permitted Colonel Stephen F. Austin of Missouri to establish a colony of Anglo-Americans on its northern frontier, in that area called Texas. Many new colonies had been formed since then. Debtors' front doors with "G.T.T."—Gone To Texas—painted on them were a not uncommon sight in the southern United States. Some friends of the Smyths in Moulton wrote George asking if he would seek out this or that person who owed them money. Scant was the hope of finding the runaways, however, and it is unlikely that George would have dared reveal their whereabouts, even if he had known. Some of these people had departed quietly at night, perhaps only hours before the storekeepers claimed their assets. They had crowded into covered wagons with pots, hoes, Bibles, and children, wrapping these things in the folds of wondrous dreams of the new country, where new land was said to really yield what it promised. It was a repetition, moved farther west, of the activities of their ancestors.

George described a population of thirty or forty thousand, including Mexicans and Indians, but with a majority of Anglo-Americans.[5] He commented that a number of settlers were indeed fugitives from Ameri-

---

[3] Winnie Allen (ed.), "The Autobiography of George W. Smyth," *Southwestern Historical Quarterly*, XXXVI (January 1933), 201.

[4] Moses K. Thomason, Moulton, Alabama, to George W. Smyth, October 24, 1831. GWS MSS, UTA.

[5] George W. Smyth, n.p., to his family, ca. 1833. GWS MSS, TSA.

can laws, but that there were good citizens as well. The better sort of Mexicans and the Anglo-American families associated freely with each other in a pleasant social atmosphere. Society was "badly organized," probably because of sparse settlement. Nearly all classes of people were represented; every person brought his own customs.[6] He said that "human nature may be seen in all its varieties from entire Nudity to genteel costume, from intelligence to beastly ignorance and From an Honorable man to the sedements of Creation."[7]

Entering Texas near the town of Nacogdoches, George had been shocked to see that even the priests participated in rowdy Mexican festivals in the streets.[8] Drunkenness and thievery were rampant among the lower classes. Nacogdoches, he wrote, was decidedly Mexican, but was what he imagined that ancient Babel had been like, with its variety of languages, for Spanish and English were by no means the only tongues spoken there. The unpleasant aspects of Texas life George attributed to the newness of everything.

If he had not found a paradise, as he admitted he had not, at least possibilities were great for a good future. The land was so rich that "cattle require no feeding. . . . Hogs require only to be kept gentle And Horses require feeding only when in actual service."[9] The land titles could not always be depended upon, but that fact was simply one of the obstacles to be overcome.

He had traveled to the rich blacklands around Austin's colony and had seen the hot prairie country of North-central Texas, but he decided finally to live in East Texas at Bevil's Settlement. Not farther than a two-day journey from Nacogdoches, the settlement had about 140 inhabitants at that time, most of them from the southern United States.[10] The countryside around Bevil's Settlement was much like that of Moulton, with sandy soil and thick forests of pine, oak, and gum. Considering the land, the excellent waterways, and the people, George was moved to pronounce it the best community in Texas.[11]

In contrast with the qualities of the land was the political situation. George wrote home giving details of the events. It seemed to Andrew a

[6] *Ibid.*

[7] George W. Smyth, Texas, to Archibald Campbell, ca. 1830. GWS MSS, UTA.

[8] Allen, "Autobiography," SHQ, pp. 201–202.

[9] George W. Smyth, Nacogdoches, Texas, to Captain Andrew Smyth, April 14, 1833. GWS MSS, TSA.

[10] Juan N. Almonte, "Statistical Report on Texas (1835)," *Southwestern Historical Quarterly,* XXVIII (January 1925), 206.

[11] George W. Smyth, n.p., to his family, ca. 1833. GWS MSS, TSA.

very exciting story. In her Federal Constitution of 1824 Mexico had set up an extravagant system of government, which was difficult, if not impossible, to administer. From the confusion that followed, factions rose and unrest prevailed. The Constitution combined the provinces of Coahuila and Texas into one state, ordering that the state make its own constitution. When the constitution of Coahuila-Texas was completed Texans were given two of the twelve representatives in the state congress, and as individuals they were guaranteed liberty, equality, property, and security if they, like all in Mexico, were Roman Catholic. In congress the colonists were at the mercy of the Mexican majority; however, the government of Coahuila was so involved with its own problems that it rather ignored Texas. Colonel Austin, leader of the American settlers in Texas, managed to stay clear of the domestic unrest.

Throughout the 1820's the United States made efforts to purchase Texas. Mexican authorities would not consider such a sale, and the tremendous flow of American immigrants, many of them determined young men like George W. Smyth, gave rise to suspicions of a great plot to take Texas by force. Ambitious young men had caused trouble in Texas before.

The settlers themselves, having worked hard to survive in the wild country, became aware of the weak voice given them in government. Sickly Coahuila, they said, was controlled by rank opportunists, who, when they thought of Texas at all, overlooked the welfare of the people and saw only a means of reaping fortunes in land speculation. The population of Texas had expanded and it seemed to the Anglo-Americans that representation in congress should be increased accordingly. The law that only a Catholic marriage was valid was resented by colonists, many of whom had been Baptists, Methodists, and Presbyterians elsewhere. Not to be disregarded was Mexico's abolition of slavery. As George explained the Mexican view in a letter home, "They have no use for slaves A Spanish Servant costs less and is more subservient to the will of his master than the African Slave."[12] Mexico, too, looked upon the abolition of slavery as a great humanitarian step forward. Slaves had been permitted in Texas only through manipulation and failure to enforce the law.

When these complaints were voiced by the colonists Mexico concluded that an American plot actually existed and took steps to strengthen its control over Texas. Abruptly in the spring of 1830, shortly after George's

[12] George W. Smyth, Bevil's Settlement, to John Gallagher, June 1, 1830. GWS MSS, UTA.

arrival, Texas was closed to further immigration from the United States. As in many of their other affairs, the Mexicans could not administer this law and Americans kept pouring across the Sabine.[13] But the whole policy served to convince Americans in Texas that their position in the government was unsure and that they should have a stronger voice in the management of their own districts. In an attempt to institute the new policy of law enforcement, Mexico established garrisons in the various Texas colonies. This move would probably not have been resented so violently had Mexico not selected convicts to man these posts. Even at that, there were localities which did not really dislike the garrisons. George made the acquaintance of the notorious Ellis P. Bean, commander of Fort Terán on the Neches River, and accepted Bean's hospitality for several weeks while learning the Spanish language.[14] Bean, an Anglo-American himself, got along well with the settlers.

But in other places, particularly at Anahuac, the Texans were so provoked that they rose against the garrisons. As a result of this, the convict soldiers were withdrawn from Texas in 1832.

By coincidence, the hostility of the settlers came at the time when Antonio López de Santa Anna was forcing himself into the presidency of Mexico. Sending flattering memorials, Texans were able to convince him that the uprisings had been in his behalf. Delighted with his willing acceptance of this, the colonists called a convention late that year and discussed sending proposals to the new Mexican leader. At a second convention in spring, 1833, the proposals were organized into petitions. From this second convention Colonel Austin was dispatched to Mexico City with the request that Texans be allowed separate statehood under the flag of Mexico. Hopes were high, for settlers were anxious to split from the inefficient government of Coahuila-Texas.

George wrote home that trouble was to come.[15] To be sure, the colonists had some grounds for complaint, but dangerous methods were being employed. He thought that the conventions had been unlawful. Like most Texans he had the utmost confidence in Colonel Austin, but he wondered whether the colonists were not expecting too much from their leader.

Andrew was impressed with his brother's knowledge of important events and the ease with which he expressed his opinion. No letter was

[13] William C. Binkley, *The Texas Revolution,* pp. 30–31.
[14] Allen, "Autobiography," SHQ, p. 206.
[15] George W. Smyth, Nacogdoches, to Captain Andrew Smyth, April 14, 1833. GWS MSS, TSA.

without some mention of that apparent Eden where George lived in the
western woods. Certainly, as far as Bevil's Settlement was concerned,
things could not have been better. A trained surveyor, George had done
considerable work in the settlement, being at first introduced by his
friend John Bevil, the old settler after whom the area was named. There
was still good land available there and George at one time suggested that
his parents join him in Bevil's Settlement.

Captain Smyth at first thought well of the idea of moving to Texas. In
that country would be a new start, a chance to have the things he had always wanted for his family. Their lot in Alabama, after all, was far short
of what he had planned for them years ago. Had Susannah lived longer
the Smyths might have sold their mill and headed west. Her death that
bitter winter made Captain Smyth weigh again the sacrifices involved in
such a move. Alone, he would have to assure the well-being of his children. Like George and Andrew, the younger children were entitled to
educations. In times like these it was important for a man to read well
and to write a good hand, however humble a mark of gentility those at-
tainments were. No local academies were to be found in Texas, nor even
schools, for that matter. George, himself, said that the people of Nacogdoches were so hard put to find a schoolmaster that they hired him, who
was certainly no teacher, to fill the post very soon after his arrival there.

Knowing that the mill on Big Nance Creek would provide a bit more
than necessities, Captain Smyth decided to remain.[16] Texas' promises
were as rich as those of Tennessee and Alabama had been years before.
Such promises were too often empty. The dreams of the old man had
waned.

The miller made his decision after Susannah's death. It was at about
the same time that he asked Andrew to write George and tell him the
"transactions" of his mother's death. Andrew had listened to his father
make plans, embellish them, and finally give them up. It was good that
his father had decided to stay in Alabama. But it was not so easy for
Andrew to surrender his own ambitions, which might well include land
in the west. For five years he had read his brother's glowing accounts of
life in that country and now he wanted to know how the opportunities
of Texas might apply to his own future. Texas was the place where men
became rich overnight. That, even above the romance of the Mexican
land, was of primary interest to the Alabama boy.

Andrew's letter reached its destination in the month of May.

[16] Andrew F. Smyth, Moulton, Alabama, to George W. Smyth, April 12, 1835.
AFS MSS.

III

George Washington Smyth was a personable man, quick to make the right friends. Those who knew him probably said that he merited the praises of his younger brother. Within a short time after his entrance into Texas he could list among his acquaintances a number of the most influential people there.

His interests varied from politics, literature, and philosophy to mathematics, which he studied in spare moments as an aid to his surveying. Nothing had benefitted him more in Texas than his education. In the settlements where he visited he came upon people who were hungry to associate with an educated man, a vestige of civilization; perhaps it was a lonely Mexican official stationed against his preference in an isolated place, or a farmer weary of reading again the small library which he had brought with him from New York and delighted to talk with someone who also enjoyed books. At home George had been instructed in the manners of polite society, and experience had refined those early lessons to give him an air of worldliness, the bearing of one who knows things.

George's conversation had a penetrating sincerity that never failed to impress people. He seldom ventured an opinion unless provoked to do so, but then the words flowed freely to the right places, making those who heard him quite certain that he had pondered the subject at length. Enough hardy backwoods merriment was mixed with George's polish to make him popular among many types of people. His friendships had led to surveying jobs, political appointments, and the ownership of land. Considering that he had been in Texas only five years, he had done better than most.

In the spring of 1834 George married Frances Mitchell Grigsby, the daughter of a Bevil's Settlement planter, who was organizing a large establishment on the Gulf prairies of the Neches River. Somewhat suspicious of the credentials of a traveler who claimed to be a Baptist preacher, Frances had insisted that the entire wedding party mount and ride to Nacogdoches so that she could marry before a priest and be sure that her marriage was valid under the laws of Mexico. No matter what the law said, most settlers, long distances from Catholic churches, were content to be married by ministers or to simply sign contracts. However, if one was particular, he had best do as Frances had done and find a priest.

A short time after his wedding George was appointed land commissioner at Nacogdoches through the influence of his Mexican friends. His personal holdings had increased to include a farm in his beloved settlement of Bevil and he considered himself a resident of that place, though he rarely stayed at home. In the friction between the small farmers and the land speculators he had taken the side of the latter, insuring a degree of prominence throughout the district. The post of land commissioner was one of significance, and George knew it. He suffered very little from his position in the speculation controversy. As he reasoned it, the question was whether to recognize land titles which were properly obtained. Texas land titles were held in low estimation in the United States as it was, and if it was decided to honor only certain ones of the titles public opinion of them would fall even more. The best solution was to limit future speculation. Because of his office he was in Nacogdoches most of the time, and it was probably there that he received Andrew's letter of April twelfth.

Writing an answer to Andrew's inquiry, George said, "I would not be understood to persuade you but I am fully persuaded you could better your situation by coming to Texas." But he added frankly that Andrew should work conscientiously to improve his penmanship and his spelling while he was at home and could go to school. Surveyors, he said, made one hundred dollars a month and since Andrew showed talent in arithmetic, he might be wise to study surveying before moving to Texas, should he decide to come.

George concluded his letter saying, ". . . you have not yet made your entrance into the busy world . . . the world is always willing to assist the young man who appears most anxious (by use of proper means) to help himself—avoid on every occasion the society of the Idle and viscious."[17] In the next three months much happened that George could write Andrew concerning political developments within Texas. History was to take surprising turns and each event was of importance to the prospective settler. Andrew wanted to know the details.

As George had feared, Colonel Austin's mission to Mexico City ended in trouble. Authorities had rejected the appeal for separate statehood. Because of a letter he had written from there in a weak moment advising his Mexican friends in San Antonio to unite with the Anglo-Americans in splitting Texas from Coahuila, Colonel Austin was arrested. Texans, although disturbed over their leader's arrest, followed the conservative policy that he had always advocated. Those who had opposed the policy of moderation in the past lost no time in forming a war party.

President Santa Anna, with a strong following, was quickly melting ob-

[17] George W. Smyth, Texas, to Andrew F. Smyth, May 22, 1835. GWS, MSS, UTA.

stacles between himself and the dictatorship of Mexico. His puppet congress declared that it could make changes in the Constitution without following the process stipulated in that instrument. Coahuila was one of two states which refused to accept this, and Santa Anna sent troops to convince it otherwise. Texans, not wanting to aid Coahuila, stayed out of the matter; soon, however, problems would reach nearer home.

Hearing that trade was being carried on through Texas ports so that Mexican tariffs could be avoided, Santa Anna ordered the reopening of the old military posts. A military commander was assigned to Texas and stationed at San Antonio. Even though the hated troops were back and the crippling laws might be enforced, the war party remained a minority. Texans were generally quiet, for to oppose the troops would be to support Coahuila.

Meanwhile, in the town of San Felipe some Texans intercepted an official messenger, and the letters he carried made it obvious that Santa Anna planned the military occupation of Texas through the local garrisons. At this discovery the war party in the San Felipe vicinity became impatient. Later that month a group of colonists, supporters of the war party, stormed and captured the military post at Anahuac, near the Gulf coast. Anahuac had been the scene of trouble before.

On the whole, Texas colonists condemned this radical action and some apologized to Mexican authorities. Meetings were held to reprimand William B. Travis, leader of the attack. Such hot-headedness as the Anahuac incident could lead only to disaster for the Anglo-Americans in Mexican domain. Mexico wanted to permanently possess this frontier of Texas and, as George noted in a letter home, the Mexicans might begin to think of Texas only in terms of a Latin American population. Mexican officers at San Antonio and in Coahuila sent circulars to assure Texans that the troops were there simply to enforce the tariff and to guard against Indians. Had George written Andrew in midsummer, 1835, he would have observed that although Colonel Austin was still detained in Mexico, his policy of moderation was the order of the day in Texas.

To deaf ears the war party begged that a consultation be assembled. This consultation, they said, could look after the welfare of Texas, since Coahuila was in such an uproar.

Bickering continued between the two factions until September, when Colonel Austin returned from Mexico, completely unaware of the situation in Texas. During his confinement he had decided that a gradual, peaceful separation from Mexico should be effected. Under Santa Anna there would never be a stable, democratic government in Texas, for he preferred using force to carry out his wishes. Before leaving Mexico City, Colonel Austin had advised the officials not to send troops to Texas.

On the trip home, however, the ship which he had taken met an armed Mexican vessel off the Texas coast. This served to convince Austin that a gradual separation might not be possible. The Mexicans were already occupying Texas and unless action could be taken at once even a peaceful severance of relations with Mexico would never be.

At home Austin endorsed the war party's idea of a consultation, which, he said, should direct the future of Texas. At first opposed to this, George changed his mind when he learned that the garrison in the city of San Antonio had been strengthened by four hundred soldiers. No longer did time exist for political maneuvering, for if given time Santa Anna would have Texas completely helpless. Colonel Austin soon stated publicly that war was the only solution.

The Consultation was scheduled to meet in October, and Austin, as chairman of the committee to collect and distribute information, issued a call for armed men. When the Consultation met, there should be force to back its decision. From all over Texas, in groups or alone, colonists went toward San Felipe, leaving farms and towns protected, in some cases, by only women and children. The Mexican commander at San Antonio ordered the citizens of Gonzales to give up the brass cannon which they had received four years earlier for protection against Indian attacks. They refused outright and troops hurried from San Antonio to take the cannon. Enlisting the support of nearby communities and passing volunteers, the people of Gonzales attacked the Mexicans and killed one. The Texas Revolution had begun.

Andrew probably had little trouble keeping informed on the Texas situation even when George failed to write. His father faithfully read the newspapers, and sometimes at night when Captain Smyth was tired, Andrew read to him at the fireside. Newspapers in the United States printed the latest word, seldom less than three weeks old, to inform a fascinated public, which identified with the Texans in philosophy and in some instances in family relationships.

Encouraged by a brother who praised Texas even in these critical times, Andrew made his decision to go. He was certain, all things taken into account, that he had chosen the correct course for himself. Late in July, 1835, he wrote George saying that the dangers of war would not keep him in Alabama "one day longer," although he had no desire to fight. Taking his brother's advice, he had been enrolled in the academy again, studying surveying, geometry, and trigonometry, and his course of study was to end on the first of October, when he would seek companions for the journey to Texas.[18] He set no certain date to leave, for the main interest before him now was his schooling.

Captain Smyth knew little of these matters before they were finally settled. And when he found out, he could at least be confident that Andrew had thought out every remote fact of the question. The miller had opposed George's move primarily because of the mysterious reputation of the new country but also because he feared that the soaring dreams of his eldest son would come to no good end. George had been away at school for such long periods of time that the miller had known him only at rare intervals during his transition to manhood. To the old man, who had endured many failures, the ideas of George W. Smyth seemed impractical and vaguely familiar—so much empty idealism gleaned from his experiences with schoolbooks.

Andrew, on the other hand, had been at home all his life. The Captain had watched him grow up, loving to work, challenging questions until he was satisfied. There was no doubt that George had been more adept in books at eighteen than his brother, but Andrew, shy and awkward socially, seemed far more able to adjust to the tough business of money-making. George's success in Texas had surprised Captain Smyth. If a man like George, suited apparently for a settled, cultured environment, could do well then it stood to reason that Andrew might do even better.

In his letter to Texas, Andrew could report that his father said he approved of the decision even though he knew that the miller wished he would stay in Alabama or nearby Tennessee. Andrew's letter was long and he took hours to write it. While the wax-sealed pages made their journey to the western woods Andrew occupied himself at the academy and at the mill.

The letter must have amused George. Andrew's handwriting, in stark contrast to that of the last letter, was an elaborate series of sweeps and swirls, arranged pretentiously around even the simplest words; so intrigued had Andrew become with writing a gentlemanly hand that his thoughts wandered over two pages in glorious avenues of words and phrases and artistic tricks with the pen and ink. He had taken to heart the suggestion that he improve his penmanship.

In closing, he added a completely candid scrawl to his sister-in-law,

[18] Andrew F. Smyth, Moulton, Alabama, to George W. Smyth, July 26, 1835. GWS MSS, UTA.

Frances: "Sister, we have not never seen each other but i am in hopes that will not bee the case many years if we both live."

By late October, 1835, word should have reached Moulton that Colonel Stephen F. Austin had temporarily left the Consultation and was leading an army on San Antonio. Adventure-hungry Americans, lured by the open hostility, rushed to Texas to fight beside the colonists. Youths in American cities, towns, and backwoods alike found a ready cause to take up in the revolt of the Texans.

At Courtland, Alabama, fourteen miles from Moulton toward the Tennessee River, seventy men formed a company, calling themselves the Red Rovers, after the red jeans they wore. They did not leave at once but remained camped on the courthouse square, drilling and making impressive preparations for their adventure. The pride of Courtland, the Red Rovers were the envy of every other little town in the entire region.

On days when he had nothing to do Andrew sometimes went to the Tennessee River by way of Courtland, so that he could watch the flatboats and keelboats, and talk to the rivermen about the places they had seen. Since Andrew had been a child the Captain had allowed him to make this little journey to the river, trusting that his love of the water would not cause him to take up the coarse habits of the rivermen.

Seven of his friends accompanied him on a trip to the river in October, and while going through Courtland they visited the town square to see the celebrated Red Rovers. Reports of their glamour had not been exaggerated, and on the rest of the trip the Moulton boys talked of nothing else. Returning from the river, they stopped again to admire the Red Rovers. By the time Andrew's seven companions were back in Moulton they had decided that they, too, were going to Texas to fight in the Revolution. Andrew, whose work at the academy had ended as scheduled, said that he would join them, if only for the trip. The Red Rovers, he realized, would have heroic experiences; maybe, as an afterthought, he could have the same.

He hastened arrangements for his departure. From the McMillan brothers, who operated the Presbyterian academy, he obtained a letter of introduction which explained the nature of his education.[19] Necessities and a few sentimental things, like the black-ribboned lock of hair, were packed into his saddlebags. Within the month he would be with his brother in Texas, a place which, in spite of the practical descriptions

<hr/>

[19] Reverend Edward McMillan and John McMillan, AB, "A Testimony in Favor of Mr. A. F. Smyth," Moulton, Alabama, October 5, 1835. AFS MSS.

George had sent, loomed very grand in his mind. The Revolution could not last long; why, if it was true that thousands of men from states like Alabama were going to help in the war, it might be over before the new year! That the war could well be over by the time he was settled in Texas suited Andrew completely. He still had misgivings about fighting in battles though he did consider the Texas Revolution a magnificent undertaking, worthy of the efforts of brave men.

Captain Smyth made sudden protests at the last minute, but he was only listened to, not heard. The miller knew not to press the point, for Andrew's mind was made up, and, after all, the trip was not really as abrupt as it seemed. He had trusted his son's judgment thus far. He had no reason to hesitate now. The sad thought remained that he, like George, might not come home again. But Andrew promised to return and the Captain knew that he would keep his word.

In an early October morning of 1835 Andrew rode away from the log mill, the only home he had ever known.[20] That last backward glimpse of the old man's tearful face, above a group of sleepy, waving children, would stay with Andrew the rest of his life. The memory was not erased even by the voices of his seven companions and the noise of the horses' hooves on the road west, to Texas.

[20] James Edmund Saunders, *Early Settlers of Alabama*, p. 66.

2. The eight horsemen went at once to the Natchez Trace, about fifty miles west of Moulton. It had taken men many years to wear this strip of wilderness into the fine road that it was. To strangers the Trace simply connected Nashville and Natchez and the places in between; but to those who lived near the road it was an outlet to anyplace, for on the Trace one could ride to the Mississippi River, and on the river float to the Gulf of Mexico, then to the sea. The Moulton travelers would only cross the Mississippi; the water route to Texas was too expensive for the youths, at least one of whom was a runaway.

I

The Trace from town to town was lonely with only an occasional plantation to break the monotony of the countryside. Mud, dust, fallen trees, and low-hanging vines plagued man and beast alike. At long intervals were inns, where space in a bed or on the floor, together with a tolerable meal, could be had, although parties of travelers found camping on a creek bank only a little less luxurious.

Away from home for the first time, Andrew Smyth may have developed misgivings about his trip when he remembered the terrible tales of the Trace which he had heard all his life. He was far from the gentle quiet of the Big Nance Creek. The silence of the Trace was dreadful, especially when one passed a ravine infamous as the site of forty murders, or a forked tree which had once held the severed head of a particularly vicious killer. Fact and legend blended so impressively in the past of the Trace that only a fool failed to keep his rifle nearby. The personality of the Trace slipped like a knife into wayfarers' minds and it was not singular that Andrew anticipated Natchez as a sanctuary, the city where the Trace came to an end.

Elegant carriages were a frequent sight among the oxcarts and wagons of Natchez, one of the most beautiful cities on the Mississippi River. A few of the houses were copied from Greek temples, in splendid detail even to the china spittoons. Andrew could hardly see enough of Natchez.

The city itself sprawled along high bluffs above the river. At the base of the bluffs, on a ledge level with the water, was the notorious water front called Natchez-under-the-Hill. Flatboats, keelboats, and fancy white steamers nosed against the wharves, loading and unloading passengers and cargo from points on the Mississippi. Because of the boats and the river atmosphere Andrew loved the Under-the-Hill section. Here people of every description moved quickly as though they had plans. Ladies of refinement always hurried from the gangplank up the bluffs, seldom lifting their veils. Gentlemen of good character descended the bluffs to transact business when necessary and left as fast as they had come. Stores and warehouses crowded beside saloons and bordellos, the sounds of business and banjos mixing into an indistinguishable jumble, which had meaning only to those who were a part of it. To the young Alabamians it was strange and new.

Many a Texas-bound revolutionist walked in the streets of Natchez, on the bluffs and Under-the-Hill. When their saddlebags were well stocked for the rough weeks ahead they ferried across the Mississippi and embarked upon El Camino Real—the storied King's Highway— for Texas.[1]

From the other side of the river, Natchez in the distance was a doll city, bobbing up here and there from the greenery on the bluffs, which themselves seemed almost to touch the clouds.

The bluffs dwindled out of sight as El Camino Real twisted through the Louisiana lowlands, an area of moist fields and black swamps. Andrew had been advised that travel through these lowlands was safe only from November until May; snakes and high water made the region nearly impassable during summer and early fall.[2] He recalled the warnings of his brother and the Natchez rivermen and found that even in mid-December this portion of the road was hazardous. After a day or so the horsemen passed into the pine barrens, which offered few hardships in comparison to the swamps.

Along the way, in settled places like Natchitoches or Alexandria, people talked seriously of the revolt in Texas. San Antonio, it was known, had fallen to the Texan forces and a government had been established by the Consultation. A former governor of Tennessee, Sam Houston, had been made commander of the Texan army. The injection of famous names like Houston into the Texas story fired Andrew's imagination. Reports were vague and sketchy, but they nonetheless provided news of the war and increased the anxiety which the Alabama travelers had felt for many weeks past.

[1] Mrs. Lipscomb Norvell, *King's Highway*, pp. 27, 280.
[2] George W. Smyth, Nacogdoches, Texas, to Captain Andrew Smyth, April 14, 1833. GWS MSS, TSA.

They followed El Camino Real through Louisiana to the Sabine River. To the promised land of Texas, this river was Jordan. Andrew led his horse from a ferry onto Texas soil, where he found himself in a country not unlike North Alabama. Odd that he had imagined it would be so different. The place seemed surprisingly peaceful to Andrew. The silence of the great woods was broken only by breezes through the pine trees.

El Camino Real changed from a yellow, sandy color to red, then deep red, as the party passed through the town of San Augustine. Within two full days Andrew and his friends were in Nacogdoches, one of Texas' famous cities, raw and strange, seeming very much a part of the wooded edge of the redlands in which it had grown up. Here Andrew got his first taste of Mexican Texas. He went to the Land Office in the government building; finding it closed and locked, he was told that his brother George had gone home to Bevil's Settlement. Not sure of what his next move should be, he camped with his friends on the outskirts of town and waited for several days.

In Nacogdoches the boys heard talk of the current conflict with Mexico from both the Mexican and the Anglo-American viewpoint. Avidly listening to the confused story unfold, each of the eight Alabama youths privately considered what his own part might be in the turbulent adventure. Andrew began to feel that the prospect of fighting in the war was more appealing than it had been.

When the people of Gonzales had defended their brass cannon and sent the Mexican detachment back to its San Antonio headquarters, Texas leaders realized that they must form an army at once. The Consultation, which would normally have seen to the organization of this army, had not yet met. To assemble the Consultation would mean many weeks' delay, for delegates, in most cases, had to travel long distances. A committee was hastily formed; a committee president was elected and Colonel Austin was placed in command of the army. Austin not a military man at all, made plans to attack San Antonio with his untrained force of men and boys. He ignored the opposing faction's efforts to point out the folly in this and proceeded to Gonzales to take command of the army.

On November 3 the Consultation met. Delegates discussed the question of complete independence from Mexico and the majority were against it. Mexico, they said, was divided within its own capital—if Texas declared independence Mexican factions would unite and sweep furiously over the revolting frontier. But the old war party shouted for a declaration of independence, gaining, for the time, a few new adherents. Colonel Austin was made one of three commissioners sent to the United States to muster support, and Sam Houston replaced him as commander of the army. The Consultation remained firmly opposed to total independence, its ideas apparent in a published defense of the colonists' actions against Mexico. When a provisional government was established the Consultation adjourned, scheduling a convention for March 1, 1836.

Colonel Austin and his two fellow commissioners left at once for the United States and the provisional government had to stand alone before a very real war.

Sam Houston was on his way to assume command of the army when a moment's inspiration fired the Texans to victory at San Antonio. Ben Milam, hero of the battle, was one of the few Texans killed, but the Mexican dead were many. Houston had opposed the siege of San Antonio, but, of course, he could not complain of the outcome. Seeing the situation as hopeless, the Mexican general surrendered and was permitted to withdraw across the Rio Grande.

The triumphant army loitered in the streets of the fallen city, unoccupied soldiers to worry the provisional government. The war was by no means over; spirits needed to be kept high. Plans for employing the army were many, but half-hearted cooperation caused a breakdown in execution. The only acceptable scheme, that of capturing Matamoros, a Mexican city on the Rio Grande, became tangled in argument and was eventually abandoned. In the next weeks troops under Francis W. Johnson quartered at Refugio contemplated marching to Matamoros; Houston manipulated for an Indian treaty and labored in opposition to the proposed Matamoros campaign; and James W. Fannin moved his men to Goliad, a town at the walls of an old Spanish mission. The forces at San Antonio were reduced. Jealous of his power, the provisional governor became so hostile toward the council that he was removed from office. And matters stood at that when Andrew crossed the Sabine and rode to Nacogdoches.

As the Texas Revolution drifted into mid-January, 1836, Texans looked unsurely around themselves. More and more it was thought that perhaps this land could best exist apart from the Mexican government.[3] To conform to Mexican ideas seemed impossible. The solution would have to come when the convention met on March 1.

With few notions about Texas remaining a part of Mexico, the volunteers arrived daily. Many passed through Nacogdoches, and if they had

[3] Stanley Siegel, *A Political History of the Texas Republic 1836–1845*, p. 29.

been there before, though most had not, they found that little change had been wrought by the war. Trade with the Indians went on as usual, as did the various transfers of land. Concern over the stability of the land titles had grown but the only real evidence of troubled times was sensed through people's conversations and perhaps through the presence of restless young men like Andrew and his companions, who were wondering what to do with themselves.

Andrew did not like this feeling; he was not used to being idle. Eagerly, the Moulton party waited for news of some action which might give them an idea of where to go. Of special interest to them was the report that the Red Rovers had made a glorious landing at Matagorda on the Texas coast.[4] The Red Rovers had come by sea. They always seemed to do things first class. Their leader was marching the entire company to Goliad to join Colonel Fannin. Word had it that every settlement along the way entertained them. The glamorous news was almost more than the Alabama boys could bear and one broke ranks. James Ellis announced to Andrew and the other six that he would ride to Goliad and meet the Rovers. He had not recovered from the scene on the Courtland square the previous October and could not see fighting this war as anything but a Red Rover.

Nothing was happening in Nacogdoches, to be sure, however, other than the fact that the Red Rovers were there, Goliad was not guaranteed to be any more exciting. Several more of Andrew's party contemplated going, too; but preferring not to humble themselves before the Courtland men, they decided to remain.

Thus, the original group of travelers lost one member, causing the remaining seven to come to quick decisions. Andrew said that he would go to his brother's house, where he was expected. The others were invited to come with him. About January 20 he told James Ellis goodbye and with his six friends rode south to Bevil's Settlement.

II

Traveling at an easy gait, Andrew Smyth probably reached his brother's house within two days. Andrew had enjoyed the free feeling of being out on his own. But in the past few days, finding Texas to be like any other place, he missed home. It would be good to be with his brother.

To George W. Smyth, Andrew was hardly less a stranger than the

4 Claude Elliot, "Alabama and the Texas Revolution," *Southwestern Historical Quarterly*, L (January 1947), 315–328.

other six from Moulton. Wren, Gregg, Thomason, Montgomery, Kaiser, McDaniel, and the absent James Ellis—their names were all familiar but the faces were new. When George had left for Texas, Andrew had been a towheaded boy of twelve. Now, a few months before his eighteenth birthday, he stood a little under six feet tall and his lanky frame suggested that he might grow even more. His hair, turned dark, hung to his shoulders. It was brushed back from a long, ruddy face memorable only for the eyes, which seemed very serious, and the irregular line of his mouth.[5] While the brothers were somewhat alike in their pale-blue eyes and chiseled features, George was certainly the better looking of the two.

Considering his own boyish attitude toward dress and carriage, together with the dust and sweat of the road, Andrew was impressed by his tall, heavy-set brother, who made a distinguished appearance in any company. They had many questions to answer, many things to talk over.

After their marriage, George had brought Frances Grigsby Smyth to this rough log cabin beside Indian Creek, in the western part of the settlement. Frances was used to better things.

In 1828 her father, Joseph Grigsby, had moved his large family, fifty slaves, and wagonloads of furniture and supplies in a caravan from Kentucky to Texas.[6] He did not say why he had left and people did not ask, for in Texas that type of information was offered, never requested. At any rate, Joseph Grigsby acquired land in Bevil's Settlement and was one of George's close friends there. It was through George's intimate association with the Grigsbys that he met and fell in love with Frances, the black-haired, blue-eyed daughter, who, for all her practical accomplishments, seemed out of place in a wilderness.

Joseph Grigsby had been in the process of moving his family and belongings to a new plantation near the Gulf coast, and in that same year of 1834 George and Frances had been married in Nacogdoches.

Not a creative woman, nor one especially interested in extending her education beyond the rudiments of reading and writing, Frances was determined in making a pleasant home for her husband. George was fortunate in finding a wife thus disposed, because his office of land commissioner made it impossible for him to look after his home or his crops regularly.

[5] Colonel John H. Burnett, 13th Texas Cavalry, to Andrew F. Smyth, May 25, 1862, discharge paper from Civil War; old photographs. AFS MSS.
[6] George Van Horn Moseley (ed.), *The Memoirs of George W. Armstrong*, p. 39.

To the isolated cabin on Indian Creek, Frances took her few pieces of fine glassware, linen, and furniture, and the two slaves, January and Drusilla, that her father had given her as wedding presents. Drusilla was so well versed in the various household arts that Frances was able to devote her time to those matters which her husband, had he been at home, would have attended to.[7] Having prospered for nearly two years, the George W. Smyths, now with an infant son, Andy, named for his grandfather, were interested in buying a new farm, building a better house.

When Andrew arrived he found his brother gravely concerned over the closing of the Land Office at Nacogdoches; going on the instructions of a single member of the Consultation, his friend Dr. Stephen Everitt, he had locked the door and come home. As it stood now, the records of property ownership in that part of East Texas were unprotected. At home he explored the possible solutions to this problem.[8] Andrew thought that the Smyths made a very splendid appearance. On this lonely creek bank they seemed far removed from the war, except of course, when George spoke of politics.

The citizens of Bevil's Settlement had pressing matters to occupy the winter of 1835 and the new year of 1836. In a climate which might vary from the extremes of light snow to scorching sun in a day's time, the settlers had learned to proceed with their business in a near disregard of the weather. By a December decree of the provisional government at San Felipe, this forty-five miles between the Sabine River and the Neches had been renamed the municipality of Jasper. The town of Jasper, which grew up around old Squire Bevil's cabin, was designated the seat of local authority. Through the poorly defined municipality were scattered several hundred people, most of them immigrants from the United States.

The twentieth day of January, in the early morning, some of those several hundred set out for Jasper to vote in the election of delegates for the March first convention. Because George had left the municipality to go to Nacogdoches to make arrangements for the protection of the land records, Andrew and his friends escorted Frances to the election-day festivities. By voting time most settlers were convinced that complete independence from Mexico was the solution to their problems.

[7] *Ibid.*
[8] Winnie Allen (ed.), "The Autobiography of George W. Smith," *Southwestern Historical Quarterly*, XXXVI (January 1933), 212–213.

Andrew mixed with the crowd in the town of Jasper, breathing the whis-key and food odors, and listening to the speakers, who now and then shouted the name of his brother through the crisp air.

One muddy street wandered beside Sandy Creek, bordered by homely log buildings. People in homespun conversed before fires, and some women smoked pipes and nursed their babies. The business of the day was of acute interest but most minds could be diverted by a well-matched fist fight, perhaps long anticipated, or by a little gambling. If the fresh pine stumps and the talk of war and Mexicans were taken away the scene would not have been different from election day in Moulton, Ala-bama, in any year that Andrew could remember.

At some late hour in the afternoon, when the ballot box was filled, the election committee retired to a secret place to count the votes. An-drew and his traveling companions were in the crowd that drew close to hear the results. The delegates were named: Dr. Stephen H. Everitt and George W. Smyth.

George returned from Nacogdoches later and was met with the news of his election.[9] In the wagon that he drove were stacked all the Land Office records, which, wisely, he was taking away for safekeeping. Loss of these documents would be hazardous to the landholder in times of such unstable government. The delegates were to assemble March 1 at Washington, a village on the banks of the Brazos River, which was a long journey from the municipality of Jasper. George and Dr. Everitt left for Washington early in February; they took the Nacogdoches Land Office records with them.

Andrew agreed to manage the farm until his services were needed with the army and then suitable arrangements would be made for the safety of the household. He wanted to stay there and be of help to his brother. The little farm really needed no overseer, for Frances was quite able to direct its operations. But Frances needed protection and Andrew needed something to do.

These weeks in Texas had been unsettled and too poorly used to please Andrew. He was accustomed to working. Wasted time made him ill at ease in such a way that he could only release himself by work. Any ideas that he had for growing rich overnight had to be put aside, for this war had set everything in confusion. Life for Andrew had always been con-sistent, so that in his plans he had simply assumed that no outside force

<hr />

[9] *Ibid.*

would come up against him. Living in an environment like the one he found in Texas was something new. Even joining the army did not appeal to him, though it seemed the opportune thing to do. He asked his friends to wait with him on Indian Creek until the time seemed right to go and fight in the war.

When mid-February came few Texans did not know that Santa Anna was nearing the Rio Grande at the head of 6,000 men. Delegates on the road to Washington pondered the matter, as did every other Texan, including Andrew, who had the responsibility of protecting a family and property. In prairie cabins men took up their rifles and from forests riders emerged, spurring their mounts toward the Texas forces. Along every main thoroughfare passed volunteers from the United States, ready for the decisive fight which had not begun.

Reactions to the political state of affairs became more pronounced in the settled areas as the delegates began to arrive at Washington-on-the-Brazos. The question was no longer what to do, but how the obvious could best be done. Weary of the peaceful municipality of Jasper, Andrew's six friends joined the volunteers on the way to the army, leaving Andrew alone with Frances, her son, and the two Negroes.

Weeks of February passed and Santa Anna reached the Rio Grande. General José Urrea was sent to attack Johnson at San Patricio. When Mexican soldiers drew near San Antonio the 150 Texas troops there barricaded themselves in an old mission compound, known as the Alamo. On the twenty-third of the month Mexican troops entered the city, demanding at once the surrender of the fortress. A cannon shot was the only reply and Mexican ammunition was turned on the Texans.

The convention met as scheduled on March 1. For a convention hall, an airy, unfinished structure of wood was selected in the town of Washington. All the delegates were not present on the opening day but the pertinent business was attended to without delay.

A declaration of independence was drafted. The delegates moved forward to sign, joined by late arrivals through the day and night. By March 4 the convention had settled down to the serious task of organizing and operating this independent nation of Texas. Sam Houston's position as leader of the army was confirmed and a plea for aid from the United States was issued. Grants of land were offered to those who would fight for Texas. Slow and always late, news of Mexican advances came to Washington—San Patricio had fallen to General Urrea, the Alamo was in great danger of the same fate. The reports were depressing.

From cramped, miserable quarters at Washington-on-the-Brazos, George found time to write to Andrew:[10]

An express arrived this morning from Bexer from Col Travis dated 3rd. Inst, the most important features of which are, that the Mexican Army under General Seizma, were variously estimated at from 1500 to 6,000 men—that reinforcement estimated at 1000 men had just arrived & from the rejoicings which were at that moment heard in the city, He judged Santa Anna himself had arrived—the Mexican Army had invested the fort (Alimo) and were entrenching at every point—The enemy kept up a constant bombardment—200 bombs had fallen in the fort, without injury to any—Our whole force in the Alimo amount only to 150 effective men—they have twenty days provisions for their present number—but ammunition scarce—Col Travis says a blood red banner waves from the Church—and Camp in token of the kind of welfare which they intend to carry on against us—he expresses his full determination to hold out to the last and sell his life as dearly as possible—

A select committee have been busily engaged in drafting a constitution which will be reported tomorrow—there has been some degree of confusion in consequence of the situation of our brave friends in the Alimo—A motion was this morning made to break up the convention and adjourn to Bexer, but it was rejected. I hope our session will be short—

The letter was sealed and sent off to Jasper.

Andrew should have sensed that George's careless handwriting evidenced his fear of what might come next. Under ordinary circumstances he took great pride in writing a beautiful hand and expressing himself elegantly. Had George known the events of that day, of the very hour in which he wrote, his concern would have deepened, for that same morning the Alamo fell before the attack of the Mexican army.

Hearing of the fate of San Patricio, Colonel James W. Fannin at Goliad sent a detachment to rescue a party of civilians from the path of the Mexicans. While these men were away from Goliad, General Houston ordered Fannin to retreat. Fannin decided to disregard the order and await the return of the detachment.

When the companies did not return by March 19, Fannin began the ordered retreat. It was too late. Urrea attacked, Fannin was forced to surrender, and with the promise of honorable treatment the Texans were marched back to Goliad. Other Texas soldiers, largely volunteers from the United States, were imprisoned with Fannin's men. On orders

[10] George W. Smyth, Washington, Texas, to Andrew F. Smyth, March 6, 1836, GWS MSS, TSA.

from Santa Anna the prisoners were led outside Goliad and shot on March 27. It was Palm Sunday.

The convention at Washington-on-the-Brazos adjourned on March 17, and George returned to his family. News of the Alamo swept Texas, at once infuriating and frightening the colonists. By the time he saw his brother again Andrew was completely involved in the Texas cause and ready to take an active part. He felt that now was the time to go to the army.

In the municipality of Jasper, as in municipalities all over Texas, a company was formed. Andrew was made First Lieutenant, probably by election.[11] This company was one of two which the municipality sent to participate in the Revolution. If the Jasper Volunteer Company had a seasoned military man for a leader it was a fact worthy of note, because in most cases the local companies were comprised entirely of farmers, with the occasional asset of a professional hunter. Planning their departure for the twenty-sixth of the month, the volunteers had time to drill with the rifle and Bowie knife and to collect provisions for the overland journey. Frances saw that Andrew's clothes and some food were packed in his saddlebags.

He saw Palm Sunday on the road with the Jasper Volunteers, completely unaware that James Ellis and the Red Rovers were dead at Goliad.[12]

On the next day, at home, George W. Smyth wrote to his father, "Texas can extricate herself from her enemies if she will do her duty but unfortunately many are disposed rather to fly from the country than to defend it."[13] When the convention had closed at Washington-on-the-Brazos many of the delegates, afraid of the Mexicans, headed toward Louisiana. They, as George had witnessed, were not alone. Women, some by themselves, some with their men, packed children and household goods into wagons and hurried to the Sabine. There it was supposed that American troops waited, lest Santa Anna bring his soldiers across the river.

During this panic of the populace, to be called the "Runaway Scrape," thunderstorms roared over the fleeing settlers, but safety had to be reached at any cost. Here and there a tea set or a fine bureau was smashed, scattered in the mud; not too many years before, those same

[11] Muster rolls of the Jasper Volunteers. Collection of Mrs. W. H. Bridges.

[12] James Edmund Saunders, *Early Settlers of Alabama*, pp. 66, 86.

[13] George W. Smyth, Bevil's Settlement, to Captain Andrew Smyth, March 17, 1836. GWS MSS, TSA.

items had been pampered on the road from Georgia or North Carolina, but today they were discarded to ease the weight of a bogged wagon.
Cabins were left empty, fields and barnyards utterly forgotten. Possessions worked for over the years were suddenly insignificant to the
frightened settlers. Fear, it seemed, had overcome all else.

The movement to the Louisiana border was a serious matter to George,
who was for all practical purposes safe at his cabin on Indian Creek. To
his father he wrote of Andrew's enlistment in the Jasper Volunteer Company, saying in conclusion, "I shall join them on the road before they
reach the army."[14] In the month or so that it took George's letter to
travel from saddlebag to schooner to riverpacket, back to a saddlebag,
and finally into his father's hands at the Moulton post office, the Texas
Revolution would come to an end. Captain Smyth would wonder just
how his sons had figured in the dramatic story.

Before midnight on March 12 Sam Houston led the army of Texas
from Gonzales eastward in retreat. Officers and common soldiers complained, for they were ready to fight and Houston, they said, was running away. But the retreat continued. Weeks passed and people began
to speculate as to what was Houston's plan. It was said that Houston
meant to lead his men across the Sabine into the United States, there to
draw Santa Anna before American gunfire. It was also said, and in some
quarters more frequently, that Houston was a coward, afraid to face
the Mexican army. Houston, himself, gave no reason, speaking only
when there was an irate officer or politician to deal with.

On March 31 Santa Anna, too, began to move to the east from his
camp at San Antonio. The two armies marched through the first days
of April, Houston working to keep his force together and Santa Anna
advancing rapidly, eager for the victory that he knew would be his.

The Jasper Volunteers, riding toward General Houston's army, were
advised that Nacogdoches was in danger. Many of these wartime rumors
came simply from the imaginations of the afraid. Risks were, nevertheless, to be avoided. Many Mexican families lived in Nacogdoches and
perhaps they could not be trusted.

Because of the possible trouble Lieutenant Andrew Smyth, with the
Jasper Volunteers, rode to Nacogdoches.[15] The streets were probably
not as full as they had been, for this city had joined in the Runaway

---

[14] *Ibid.*
[15] Muster rolls and microfilm information on the Jasper Volunteers. Collection of Mrs. W. H. Bridges.

Scrape. It must have seemed as peaceful as always to Andrew. Some of the Mexican families which George had written home about several years before had gone for good to Mexico or perhaps to New Orleans. Those citizens who remained were aware of Houston's retreat—the movement was considered either rank cowardice or part of a great secret plan. No one knew and the most recent information was rather old. Confusion was mingled with terror of what the future might hold. Texans had much to lose.

Houston's men were still disgruntled and restless; a number of them had deserted; and others were ill with measles and mumps. Texans had 920 to 1,000 men in their army, while Santa Anna would command, with the arrival of General Martín Perfecto de Cós, 1,300. Houston was well over one hundred miles from the Sabine River and Santa Anna was dangerously near.

On April 20 the two armies moved into position near Lynch's Ferry on the San Jacinto River. During the afternoon of the next day the Mexicans enjoyed their siesta, with no idea that the Texans had slipped quietly into the underbrush nearby. Some of the Mexican posts were unguarded, and in the final moments of the siesta cries of "REMEMBER THE ALAMO! REMEMBER GOLIAD!" crashed through the silence. Santa Anna's army scattered about grasping for bayonets and equipment in an air of total confusion filled with screams and explosions.

The battle lasted eighteen minutes. Almost half the Mexicans were dead; Texans could hardly notice their losses. Santa Anna disguised himself and fled, only to be captured the next day by a Texas soldier, who had no idea that his prize was the President of Mexico.

III

At about the time that the Jasper Volunteer Company received word of the Texan victory at San Jacinto and the end of the Revolution, it was given orders to report at Harrisburg as soon as possible. Harrisburg had succeeded Washington-on-the-Brazos for a short time as the seat of government, and though the capital was now at Velasco on the coast Harrisburg was in the vicinity of the battlefield of San Jacinto and much in the center of activity.

Andrew made the tiresome march to Harrisburg, where he joined the main body of the Texas army. Because he had spent the most eventful days of the Revolution calmly in Nacogdoches, it was exciting for

Andrew to mix among the soldiers of San Jacinto and hear the tales they had to tell. May 8, the day after his arrival, he wrote George:[16]

... we are all encamped here now but will take up the line of March to the west on tomorrow. our cavalry is now on the persuit of the Mexican troops to keep them from carrying off stock and other property. I expect you have heard of Houston's great victory before this time ... our brave heroes attacked Santa Anna and fifteen hundred of his chois troops.

The Mexican army, in accordance with the terms of the Treaty of Velasco, was permitted to cross the Rio Grande. Andrew followed them all the way, in company with the troops assigned to that mission.

At the Rio Grande the Jasper Volunteer Company disbanded and Andrew was once again a civilian. He was glad to be through with the war. The Red Rovers and James Ellis had been slain, he knew, at Goliad; the tragedy of war had come very close to him and it could have come closer. James Ellis, had he stayed away from Goliad, would probably be traveling home now, to Moulton. During lags in conversation on the road Andrew thought about how his Texas adventure had turned out so far. It had not been the pleasure excursion that he had expected.

Elsewhere in Texas, Andrew's six companions discussed the same thing on the way to El Camino Real.[17] In looking back they felt fortunate indeed not to be beside James Ellis in a grave somewhere in this wild country. But in spite of the sad memory which mention of the Revolution would always bring, in spite of the criticisms that he daily heard of the wilderness, Andrew was still ready to give his luck a try. Maybe the bad part was over. He rode across the prairies and then into the western woods, where he slowed his horse and let his eyes play on the good countryside of the municipality of Jasper. It seemed that he was home.

[16] Andrew F. Smyth, Harrisburg, Texas, to George W. Smyth, May 8, 1836. GWS MSS, UTA.
[17] Saunders, *Early Settlers of Alabama,* pp. 66, 86, 112.

3. Andrew's military career, if brief, gave him a sense of identity with the new Republic of Texas. The excitement of revolution relaxed; he could consider his new home, the municipality of Jasper. The Neches and Angelina Rivers on the west and the Sabine River on the east offered direct water routes to the Gulf of Mexico, and thus were outlets to the rest of the world. Andrew liked being near good rivers, especially since he thought of them as passages to any place where he might want to go. That the rivers led to the Gulf coast was the only real concern of the municipality of Jasper, for the rest of the world, which might appeal to a dreaming youth, was of little interest to the backwoodsmen. They had enough at home to occupy their time.

I

The hilly country between the rivers was yet untamed. Crops still grew around persistent stumps, and roads meandered to avoid natural obstructions. Forests of beech, sweet gum, sycamore, oak, and the predominant pine were so thick that the trees grew tall and slender in an effort to reach the sunlight. Trees were everywhere, literally, but of all the trees the magnolia made this area different. It grew more abundantly here than it did in other parts of Texas. Had it not been for the magnolia and its pristine white blossoms, the countryside, during the summer months, would have seemed monotonous. Even at that, some travelers complained that the miles and miles of unbroken forest depressed them.

Spring-fed creeks provided excellent water, making wells often quite unnecessary. In swamps stagnant pools reflected cypress trees and Spanish moss, and shimmered, dark and moist, in contrast with the green hills nearby. Of the seasons, spring was the most beautiful. Then the shadowed woods were dappled with dogwood, May apple, honeysuckle, and the wildflowers of azalea, violet, and cherry. By May the woods flowers were gone, but the magnolia bloomed until fall.

Fine farms could be envisioned from the soil. The land was rich, well suited to planting, with only one conspicuous problem—that of clearing away the trees, which did not seem so great a task to Andrew, who made plans as his horse jogged along. Before a man established himself he could live on game. Wild animals, even an occasional bear, roamed the hills and canebreaks just waiting to be transformed into one of those strange frontier dishes that all Texans knew about.

Optimistically, Andrew ignored the mud and mosquitoes and briars, thinking that prospects for his future were very good indeed.

Once dismounted at the cabin on Indian Creek, Andrew was no doubt surprised to learn that George and Frances had recently returned from the Louisiana border. During the panic of April, rumors had floated through these woods saying that Santa Anna was camped not far from this section and that he was marching soon to Nacogdoches. Many of the local settlers hurried to the Sabine. It would have been hard to convince the people of Jasper that Santa Anna was uninterested in their farms.

Left alone in the Indian Creek area, George W. Smyth had succumbed to the silence and the howl of the wind in the pines. He quickly reasoned that his first duty was to his family; he packed his household goods, his family, and his slaves into wagons, and rushed to join his neighbors across the river.[1] How much he wished that he had in his hands the letter which Captain Smyth was showing proudly in Alabama. Of course, he had had himself to think of, too; Mexicans were supposed to be cruel to enemy politicians and his name, after all, was on the Declaration of Independence.

George was probably not proud of his actions, considering that the Mexicans had come nowhere near Jasper, but, regardless, he had irons in the fire, things to be done in the months ahead.

It seemed odd to Andrew that his brother had run away from the war. He rationalized, however, that if he had been in the same position, with a family to consider, he would have done the same thing. At any rate, he did not dwell upon the subject, for George had outlined a course of study in surveying as it applied to Texas, and Andrew set to work on it.[2] Frances provided a place for him in the cabin. Very seriously he undertook the lessons, allowing only farm duties and an occasional part-time surveying job to interfere. George was very kind in steering the jobs his way, but these studies were of the first importance. All that he learned he stored away to use when the time was right. To keep things which might be of use later on was a trait distinctly part of his make-up.

Wounded at the Battle of San Jacinto, Sam Houston sailed to New Orleans for medical treatment. Much of the Texas army still looked

---

[1] L. W. Kemp, *The Signers of the Texas Declaration of Independence,* p. 323.
[2] George W. Smyth, Nacogdoches, Texas, to Andrew F. Smyth, December 6, 1836. GWS MSS, UTA.

with scorn upon the General, saying that he was cowardly and had been forced to fight the Mexicans when further retreat seemed impossible.

While some soldiers still ridiculed him, New Orleans welcomed him as a hero, the liberator of Texas. The men and women of the Runaway Scrape came home again, dazzled by San Jacinto, to applaud their General. Impressive reports of the New Orleans reception increased his popularity.[3]

On his way from New Orleans to San Augustine, Houston spent a night in Jasper, where a ball was held in his honor. Sufficient advance notice had been given for the ball to be a very large affair with guests coming from as far away as Nacogdoches. If the General's courtly manners and stylish brocades won Andrew's admiration, it was nothing unusual. Sam Houston was a man to remember. And Andrew, that evening in the setting of candles and greenery, hardly noticed the log walls of the room and his homespun suit, but imagined that someday he, like the General, might be courtly in broadcloth and pearl buttons.

In mid-August the voters of San Augustine sent a memorial to Jasper announcing their nomination of Houston for president of the Republic.[4] It was not long before he had won the election over his two opponents, one being Colonel Austin. The President selected his cabinet, wisely making the heartbroken Austin secretary of state.

Problems loomed before the government: Santa Anna was a prisoner of war to be dealt with; the Mexicans hungered for revenge; possible annexation by the United States was to be argued; and unoccupied young males waited for grants of land, the promised reward for service in the Texas Revolution. Not least to be considered was whether the world would recognize the new Republic of Texas.

Andrew, a Texan less than one year, did not fully realize the importance of these things to his well-being. George talked politics at the cabin all the time but Andrew was interested in other things. The Revolution and the ball at Jasper over, he discarded political thoughts like a child might discard a toy which had become boring.

On their farm the Smyths had prospered. George had now acquired a much larger tract of land on Walnut Run, fronting on the Neches River in the southern part of the municipality. It was rich land that bordered ice-blue Walnut Run, the county's finest creek. If Andrew was looking for work, he could find more than his share in helping establish this new farm.

[3] Marquis James, *The Raven: A Biography of Sam Houston,* pp. 258–259.
[4] Stanley Siegel, *A Political History of the Texas Republic, 1836–1845,* p. 51.

Near the present farm on Indian Creek was the Angelina River village of Bevil, the center of the municipality's river transactions. For some time now Andrew had been riding to the mouth of the Neches to see that George's ordered merchandise from New Orleans and Galveston was properly protected before being transferred to a keelboat for the journey upriver to Bevil.[5] These river trips were a joy to Andrew and on two occasions he and his horse rode back to the municipality as keelboat passengers.

George had ordered long lists of items, both for the new household and for farming. Because the new farm was about ten miles below the point where the Angelina emptied into the Neches, George had to transfer his river business to a private landing, which he built on his own land on the Neches River, at the mouth of Walnut Run. Even though it was desirable to be near the shipping center at Bevil, the new land was better suited to planting than the Indian Creek farm had been.

Andrew decided to remain with his brother, at least until the new farm was established. He admitted in a letter to his father that he wanted a business of his own but did not know exactly where to begin.[6] The Captain's warnings had perhaps made him afraid of the possibility of a mistake.

George, Andrew, and the slave, January, loaded a wagon with provisions and camped on the new property twelve miles away. Under the constitution of the Republic, George, having resided in Texas prior to the Revolution, was granted this "League and Labor" of land—4,605 acres—as "head of a family." The George W. Smyth headright would require many weeks of hard work before it could be considered even slightly improved, much less a farm. On an elevation near Walnut Run, space was reserved for a residence. From there in three directions fields would extend and run for some distance along the banks of the creek.

In fall, 1836, one Benjamin Allen began building a residence which George had contracted and paid fifty dollars for months earlier.[7] Originally he had wanted the house placed beside Indian Creek but that was before the Walnut Run property had come into his hands. In the clearing away of woods, the straight trees were given to Allen for use in the house, trees of lesser quality burned or split for rail fences. The clearing

[5] Andrew F. Smyth, Georgia, Texas, to George W. Smyth, November 27, 1836. GWS MSS, UTA.

[6] Andrew F. Smyth, Bevil, Texas, probably to his father, 1837. AFS MSS.

[7] Benjamin Allen, Jasper, Texas, to George W. Smyth, March 23, 1836. GWS MSS, UTA.

of fields was well along, in December, when Frances, little Andy, and the servant, Drusilla, moved into the new house.[8] A comfortable place in the house was assigned to Andrew.

Before the servants' houses and the remainder of the farm buildings were built the Smyths found time to look over what they had done. Had Andrew written his father and described the new house, he would probably have been enthusiastic. From a distance the new house seemed very fine, indeed, particularly to those who had so patiently watched each log fitted into place through the chilly and often rainy weeks of the past two months. It was of roughhewn logs, somewhat like the old cabin, though bigger and stronger, consisting of two rooms separated by a covered breezeway, with a vast loft above. The chimneys were pine frames covered with clay that had been mixed with Spanish moss and straw, and the floors were split logs placed flat side up. Walls and floors had the fragrance of wood, freshly cut and briefly seasoned.

In the new fields, which stretched from the residence and stopped abruptly at tall walls of forest, little fires glowed around hundreds of stumps. Their glow in the dark of night made it seem that some strange, gorgeous constellation had been born among the clods of the new-broken ground. These fires would be tended constantly until all the stumps and roots were gone and the earth was ready for spring planting.

II

The Republic of Texas existed through the months of 1837; its sire, Colonel Austin, was dead, and its President was somewhat more troubled about his own private life than the problems of the Republic. In the new capital, Houston, near Harrisburg and the San Jacinto Battlefield, government officials divided their time between political intrigue and the pursuit of fortunes in land. Patterned after that of the United States, the government system was not efficiently operated, nor was the money available to make it so.

Many times dissatisfaction came to the surface. The tale is told of a cantankerous squire on the riverbank southwest of Jasper. This squire disliked Sam Houston and felt that his community could best exist in its own republic. His neighbors listened. Several farms were thrown together under the presidency of the squire and withdrew from the Republic

[8] Winnie Allen (ed.), "The Autobiography of George W. Smith," *Southwestern Historical Quarterly*, XXXVI (January 1933), 213.

of Texas. President Houston, on an East Texas visit, came and met with
the old man in a neutral cornfield and argued to no avail. At last it was
proposed that a round of poker decide the issue. The squire was pas-
sionately devoted to card games. Houston produced the victorious hand;
the squire, a man of his word, disbanded his little republic forever.[9]

In the face of such feelings Texas was experiencing a vast wave of
immigration which had started at the close of the Revolution—land
under the Republic seemed a safer investment than that which Mexico
had offered earlier. Opportunities were to be had for married men and
bachelors, alike. Andrew, for example, was granted 320 acres on the
Angelina River for his services in the army.[10] It was well-timbered land,
which to Andrew probably seemed useless at the moment. Nevertheless,
he now owned land and for an instant felt very secure.

Thousands of grants were made under similar circumstances. In some
cases old settlers moved to new locations within Texas on land grants
or large purchases that they had made. George's father-in-law, Joseph
Grigsby, had been in the process of moving to the Gulf Coast prairies
for several years, and now, in the first of 1837, he turned his Jasper holdings over to a son and applied himself to completing his large-scale plantation operation at a spot on the Neches, soon to be called Grigsby's
Bluff. Although civilization in the Republic could be envisioned only
dimly from the forests and prairies, the times went fast. Wearing deep
roads where there had been none before, the optimistic moved on, determined to make each hour count.

The constitution of the Republic stipulated that "Convenient Counties" be made from the earlier divisions of the country; consequently,
the municipality of Jasper became Jasper County. As the county seat,
the town of Jasper kept its name; and Bevil, on the Angelina, was renamed Bevilport. Before Jasper County could be officially born, definite
boundary lines had to be formulated and presented for approval to the
congress of the Republic.

When the commissioners met to select minor officers, they knew that
a county surveyor was needed at once. Andrew attended their meeting
and presented his letter of recommendation from the Presbyterian acad-

[9] This was a popular tale, told for many years in East Texas. The particular
version used here was told to William Seale, Sr., in about 1900 by Emily Allen
Smyth. Seale to author, spring, 1961.

[10] Land Commissioner Jerry Sadler, Austin, Texas, to author, July 19, 1962.
Duplicate to the land certificate.

emy in Moulton. His brother was one of the commissioners and that fact, of course, helped win the appointment.[11] Since George's surveying equipment was not in use at the time and Andrew had none of his own, it was made available for the project. Andrew and his two assistants packed only the barest provisions and went on their way.

Months were required to finish the job—woods, swamps, and insects competed with the elements to break their spirits, while each day the surveyor's transit required a touch so soft that it seemed absurd in light of the rawness of everything else. At difficult moments Andrew lost his patience and flew into rages in the vast, quiet forest, but only his assistants were affected by these outbursts. Now and then a cabin might welcome the surveying party, just to hear new voices. A night spent under a roof was pure luxury, for more often some pine thicket or dry place in the swampland sheltered them.

Andrew made a small salary from the job and if it was not substantial, it was, at least, cash money. A good job done for the county, moreover, might mean better paying private contracts later on, a prospect that compensated for the low wages. He would save as much money as he could, so that when the opportunity came to invest, say, in a farm or store, he would have something to spend.

When he left Alabama, he had had a general idea, well formed, of what he wanted to do in Texas. Now he was not sure.

From time to time his thoughts turned to the river life that he had loved as a boy and had never gotten out of his ambitions. He liked the water, its sound, and its mystery; he liked the way it made a clean sweep of everything in its way, a passage to where it was going. Rivermen had seemed like guests of the water, profiting from their use of it, though, as the Negroes said, keeping a respectful manner about them, if only while they were on the river. Farmers seemed to be the money makers in Texas. Perhaps he should farm. For sure, he had ample time to think about these matters on the long surveying excursion. By December the boundaries were established, and on the twelfth of the month President Houston signed his name to the document officially proclaiming the county of Jasper.

Since his discharge from the army Andrew had found a new friend in Joseph Grigsby. Visiting with him and his wife, Sally, at their home on the Neches, the lanky, shy youth enjoyed the old couple, who appreciated an occasional bottle of wine and amusing company. There on the

---

[11] George W. Smyth, Jasper, Texas, to Andrew F. Smyth, October, 1837; fragments of field notes mentioning the Sabine and Neches Rivers. AFS MSS.

windswept porches overlooking the river they talked, the three of them, in fall afternoons before the cold weather drove them inside to the fire. Joseph was fond of Andrew and was responsible for his first job in Texas that was independent of his brother's influence. Whenever he was not needed at the Walnut Run farm Andrew liked to go to Grigsby's Bluff. Joseph Grigsby was about the same age as Andrew's father, but Joseph's hard life had led to an old age of wealth and to the occasional moments of leisure which Captain Smyth would probably never have. The friendship had been good for Andrew.

While Andrew was doing preliminary work on the boundaries of Jasper County, Joseph wrote George saying that Jefferson County, which included Grigsby's Bluff, needed a surveyor. After his work in Jasper was finished Andrew made the eighty-mile trip to his friend's house and found that Joseph had the commission set aside for him.[12]

Most of Andrew's work as Jefferson County's surveyor centered in the new town of Beaumont, located on a bend in the Neches, upriver from Joseph's house, where Andrew lived during this time. He was in Jefferson County for a few months less than a full year. Although he never fully set down the reasons for his resignation, Andrew probably did not like being a civil employee in such a new place, where his only friends were so much more advanced socially and financially than he that he could do nothing for them, while they could do everything for him, and did. This situation, he knew, would be worse as the county became more settled. At George's he had to be more than a guest in the house; from the time of Andrew's arrival George had given him responsibilities and had expected the best results. In Jasper County he had met many people and had made many friends. This was something which he did not find easy to accomplish in the first place. Too, Jasper County was by no means well enough settled that an enterprising young man could not hope to make a place for himself there. Andrew was not like George, who could move with few regrets each year if the new situation bettered him greatly. He missed East Texas now, as he had missed Moulton when he first crossed the Sabine. The advantages of staying in Jefferson County were not great enough to keep him there. March 10, 1838, he submitted his resignation at Beaumont and returned upriver to Jasper.[13]

[12] Joseph Grigsby, Grigsby's Bluff, Texas, to George W. Smyth, January 14, 1837. GWS MSS, UTA.

[13] Andrew F. Smyth, Beaumont, Texas, to the Jefferson County Commissioners, March 10, 1838. AFS MSS.

In addition to the 320 acres that he had received for service in the Texas army, Andrew was eligible for another grant of land through the headright provisions in the Constitution. As a single man over seventeen who had been in Texas prior to the break with Mexico, he was entitled to one third of a league of public land.

On the way upriver from Beaumont he was advised of available property in Liberty County, located across the Neches River from Jasper County. The spot that he decided upon was situated twelve miles downriver from Bevilport and was on the banks of the Neches, not far from George's river landing at the mouth of Walnut Run. During June the land lines were marked; to reduce the cost of surveying his land, Andrew served as assistant to Dan Hoit, the official surveyor of the county. October 26, 1838, Mr. Hoit was paid twenty-five dollars for his services and the Andrew F. Smyth headright was recorded.[14]

That place on the Neches was a fine one. When the timber was cut away perhaps a good farm could be developed. The 320-acre plot on the Angelina in Jasper County was eight miles above Bevilport. The Angelina joined the Neches one mile below that town, making the upriver grant almost as valuable as the one farther down.

Remembering the unsure future that had faced him in Alabama three years before, Andrew could now feel very close to success. But to him, as to thousands of other Texans, it only seemed close. He had not the money to make a farm from his land nor to buy slaves to work the fields. His 1,796 acres had yet to yield a livelihood.

[14] Daniel Hoit, Liberty County, Texas, to Andrew F. Smyth, October 26, 1838. AFS MSS.

4. Living again with his brother on Walnut Run, Andrew assumed some of the responsibilities of the farm. But since George relished being at home and fancied himself a country squire, Andrew had time to take small surveying jobs and become acquainted with this part of East Texas, which he had come to think of as home.

I

On the way from George's house to town were a number of farms where Andrew could stop for a refreshing gourd of water and perhaps a sausage and a cold biscuit; at mealtime the passer-by was always asked to "break bread," which might include four kinds of meat, hot vegetables, cornbread, a dessert of sweet-potato pie, and, if the family was not financially ahead, sassafras tea instead of coffee. In the company of the hardy, outspoken farmers Andrew lost some of his timidity. He was even known to call upon a few of them because of their pretty daughters.[1]

To the farmers there was no life but that of planting the land, and of course the logical step for Andrew seemed to be the clearing of his river property for a farm. But he found himself riding again and again down to Bevilport to talk with the rivermen of the Angelina and the Neches, just as he had as a child visited with the rivermen of the Tennessee. All his life he had depended in some way upon water for his welfare. Big Nance Creek had determined his family's monetary status from year to year; even now the rivers that served Jasper County brought in supplies for the Walnut Run place and rose so high at times that surveying expeditions had to be postponed. Rivermen got their pay in cash and worried less about the crops, because even if there was no cotton to ship downriver, there were goods which they could bring back to the planters and storekeepers. Andrew liked this approach to money-making, which seemed more nearly foolproof than the farmer's life.

Working at George's farm he had gained valuable knowledge of the arts of husbandry, the most of which both George and Andrew had learned from the slave January, whom Joseph Grigsby had wisely presented to his daughter. To discard this accomplishment in favor of fol-

---

[1] M. Constantine Smyth, Mooresville, Alabama, to Andrew F. Smyth, December [?], 1856. AFS MSS.

lowing a career on the river, which he knew nothing about, would be impractical. Surveying was not what Andrew wanted for a life's work, either, for the surveyor had to follow new land if he expected regular employment. And Andrew wanted to stay in Jasper County. The present situation, however, would not do for long; he was like a guest in his brother's house, a child laboring as a farm helper because he thought he should, but feeling very useless to himself. The older he grew the more he wanted a free life, completely his own.

Soon enough George appeared with a proposition which eased the situation, if only temporarily.

George W. Smyth had given most of his time to the Walnut Run farm since the Revolution. Beginning on a small scale, he had expanded each year, until now, early in 1839, he had many acres in cultivation and had bought several more slaves for his labor force. Although farming was George's livelihood, it was not first in his thoughts, no matter how hard he tried to make it seem so. When the opportunity presented itself he bought books so that his studies could be continued. Along the log walls of his house were lined volumes on mathematics, natural science, history, and works in English literature. During his residence there Andrew had hardly opened so much as one book. He was amazed that his brother could devour more reading matter than he could keep supplied with. In addition to this, George's interest in politics was still very much alive— he knew that today's informed neighbor was often tomorrow's office holder.

Frances was delighted with her husband's various pursuits and, to help him, participated tactfully in the management of the farm. At George's side she attended church meetings and barbecues; he had spoken of their "common destiny" and to achieve the best she eagerly contributed her share.[2] The first great tragedy in their marriage had occurred in 1837, when little Andy died. George and Frances could not be consoled. Andrew, according to instructions, selected a place near the house on the banks of Walnut Run for a cemetery and planted it with myrtle trees; January built a coffin of pine and the child was buried there. Since then a daughter, Sarah, had been born. The new baby drew George and Frances from months of grief and the routine of the Walnut Run farm gradually returned.

In the long period that George and Frances had spent secluded from

[2] Winnie Allen (ed.), "The Autobiography of George W. Smyth," *Southwestern Historical Quarterly*, XXXVI (January 1933), 203.

everyone Andrew managed the farm. He went there out of a sense of duty, but at the same time he understood their sorrow and wanted to help.

The farm was no longer a small operation. It required undivided attention. When a Negro was acquired a house had to be built for him, and, eternally, new fields needed to be cleared. Repairs were required here and there. Such a thing as organization was a dream, for new duties came with each hour. Frances, usually a great help in her husband's farm work, was pregnant, expecting her third child in the fall. Drusilla was so busy attending to the housework, Sarah, and her mistress, that even the matter of clothing for the slaves fell upon George. Because he could not manage everything by himself and still see to his intellectual interests he asked Andrew to assist him at least until summer. The offer was satisfactory. Andrew was trying to select the business that he wanted to enter and working with his brother, while not really profitable, would give him a few more months in which to weigh the possibilities. And, of course, there was the sense of duty which he felt toward this brother who had always insisted upon sharing all that he had with Andrew.

In accordance with the constitution of the Republic, Sam Houston did not succeed himself as president. Mirabeau B. Lamar had won the election and had been inaugurated in December, 1838. Among the problems which Lamar had to deal with was that of establishing a boundary between the United States and Texas along the Sabine River. George was invited to handle the project in the capacity of chief surveyor. He did not want to refuse the offer and would hardly have done so under any circumstances, but he needed to make arrangements for his holdings on Walnut Run. It was finally decided that Andrew become overseer of the farm, working in exchange for a stipulated portion of the crop.[3] This position changed his stature greatly in the neighborhood, but most of all, in his own eyes.

Appointed on May 13, George left during the summer. Andrew immediately assumed the responsibility of the busy establishment, its Negroes, its records, and the plans already made for its improvement. It was a fine job for a young man to have. In the months of spring he had still arrived at no decisive ideas for his future, but being overseer of a large farm would give him a higher place among the businessmen of the area and a good, respectable spot from which to look around.

[3] Farm notes on the Walnut Run place. AFS MSS.

II

The people of Jasper County became well established under the Republic of Texas. Cotton was raised there with corn and the various garden products, bringing abundance to the farmers and trade to the storekeepers. To avoid high duties Texas cotton was sometimes smuggled across the Sabine into the United States, where brokers waited for it—some Jasper County people undoubtedly participated in this since it was such a short trip to the Sabine from their fields.

The town of Jasper had about fifteen log houses, a surprising number to visitors, who because of the trees could count but a few from the street.[4] Bevilport was growing slowly, depending upon occasional flatboats and keelboats to bring trade. Most of the inhabitants of the county were farmers, "good backwoodsmen," who went into Jasper on court days and who rode to Bevilport to sell what they had harvested at home.[5] A substantial number of farmers used the Sabine to transport their cotton, but Andrew rarely saw these men of the eastern part of the county. The farms were little empires within themselves, providing food and clothing for those who ran them.

On the farm beside Walnut Run, Andrew saw to the planting of cotton and corn, more than likely working beside the Negroes in the field. George came home whenever he could on brief visits of a week or less. Anything that was wanted could usually be made on the spot, but sometimes Andrew needed to go into town for supplies. If Jasper had nothing he might try Dr. Stephen Everitt's store in Bevilport; if he met with no luck there he could put a skiff in the river at George's farm and go to Town Bluff over in Liberty County, not far from his own Neches River land.

Essentially the towns in the region were in the same predicament: all export and too little import. A traveler through Jasper in 1839 was greeted by a Negro on the road who joked that "only bad whiskey was to be had in Jasper," which about summed up the situation.[6]

Luxuries were almost unheard of. Not many years before, when settlers demanded less of prosperity, substitutes had been made for things not available. As it was now, men and women who had worked hard wanted pretty things, indeed, simple items which they had taken

[4] Max Freund (ed. and trans.), *Gustav Dresel's Houston Journal: Adventures in North America and Texas, 1837–1841*, p. 60.
[5] *Ibid.*, p. 61.
[6] *Ibid.*, p. 60.

for granted back in the United States. The farmer might hope someday to get a store-bought silk vest from Galveston, though for him to even order an iron stove with which to heat his parlor was presumptuous.

Small wagon trains and keelboats made their way to Jasper County now and then but the people fought so for the merchandise that it disappeared before most of the populace knew that it was available. Storekeepers hired the few keelboatmen that came upriver to bring goods for their business houses in Bevilport or Jasper and at best the stores did not offer an interesting stock. Andrew once spent two months at the mouth of the Neches River trying to gain space aboard a keelboat for some supplies for the Walnut Run farm; until he finally found one, he was told that the merchants upriver had hired all the boats.[7] A dependable means of using the river, both for importing and exporting, was needed.

George's boundary surveying was finished early in 1840, and, as had seemed probable, he was appointed to represent the Republic in a meeting with United States officials regarding the boundary line. As commissioner he was away from home for a year, finally returning in September, 1841.[8]

The capital of Texas was now the town of Austin, about 250 miles from Jasper toward San Antonio. George had seen this new capital when he submitted his reports. President Lamar's administration was coming to a close and it was obvious that Sam Houston would be the next president. Lamar's hostile attitude toward the Indian tribes had precipitated attacks on settlers and general unrest in those areas near Indian country. The Republic was still as debt-ridden, if not more so, but in time it could at least claim that Great Britain, France, and Belgium had joined the United States in recognizing Texas' independence. Everything from the Indian question to the program for public schools had found its way into Congress.

Back on Walnut Run neighbors could be entertained for hours with stories of the new capital, the recent boundary negotiations, and such personalities as Mirabeau B. Lamar and the celebrated Tennessean, Judge John Overton, who had accompanied George on the surveying expedition as the United States envoy.

George wrote his father that without Andrew's loyal attention to the "Jasper County holdings" he would not have been able to afford the "extravagance of public service." Amiable and dignified, George had

[7] Andrew F. Smyth, Grigsby's Bluff, Texas, to George W. Smyth, August 21, 1839. AFS MSS.
[8] Allen, "Autobiography," *SHQ*, p. 213.

made an impression in the mind and conversation of his region. When this or that event had taken place, he, the backwoodsmen said, had been right there participating or certainly within listening distance. Being considered a first citizen had its advantages.

Andrew, uninterested in a public career, had been a good overseer. His frugal management had made the farm stride forward. He had learned fast. Cotton, corn, and a little tobacco were planted each spring, harvested, and what was not used at home was sold, probably to the agent at Bevilport who represented an exporter in one of the coastal cities. Some of the farmers dealt directly with the factory at Galveston or New Orleans, but, in any event, the planter was responsible for shipping his cotton to the warehouse of the buyer.[9] Andrew grew accustomed to his position and now that George was at home to stay more extensive projects could begin. Following the process that his brother had established, Andrew extended the fields each year. The farm was now far-reaching although forests still covered most of the Smyth headright. The Smyths had been fortunate in this Republic, where most farms were not so prosperous. It seemed that some people expected the land to make a living for them.[10] To open a large farm required a big labor force all at once, and, without slaves or many sons, a settler might find this too much of a hardship.

Towns were quite alive, but good times had yet to come to most of them. Houston, for instance, having lost the capital to Austin, was in a decline. In land speculating or importing and exporting, some men had made fortunes; this was contrary to the rule. The great movement of Americans to the Republic continued as before and the gaudy optimism of Texans fought to push aside disillusionment. Recalling failure in the United States, settlers were under pressure not to give up easily but to anticipate the good times that their labors under the Lone Star might bring.

Typical were the ambitious plans for the Walnut Run farm: orchards would be planted in a certain high place; new pastures would be cleared toward the river; and the house would be enlarged and modernized, when there was time. For these projects Andrew stayed on as overseer, a job which his brother relied upon him to fill.

Although he had been a competent manager and now had some money to spend, farming had little real appeal to Andrew. In the past

[9] Andrew F. Smyth account books for 1839 and 1840. AFS MSS.
[10] William Ransom Hogan, *The Texas Republic: A Social and Economic History*, pp. 81–109.

three years he had seen the need of the backwoods for imported goods and had wondered why this need was not filled sufficiently.[11] The Neches and the Angelina were navigable, but very few flatboats and keelboats could be found as far upriver as the Walnut Run landing or Bevilport. Such was not the case on the Sabine, which, despite the inconvenience, was getting some patronage from the western part of the county. Stores in Jasper and Bevilport and Town Bluff required merchandise on, of course, a larger scale than did any individual in the county.[12]

The people of the vicinity had been so long removed from luxuries that they could do without them and yet the storekeepers did a thriving business, for when a customer saw good things on display he wanted them at once. In turn, the sudden halt in a supply of, say, calico, an important product, was a near disaster—the calico had been available for perhaps only three months, but already it had become a necessity for the buying public. It was odd, Andrew noted, that so few rivermen took a sober interest in making money in Neches and Angelina trade. A large consumer in behalf of his brother's farm, Andrew watched this problem build up.

With no slaves, Andrew knew that it would take a long time to convert his wilderness land into a paying farm. And he really did not want to be a farmer—to work hard, then stop and sit on a porch, waiting to see if the weather would be kind enough to let him make a crop. For years all profits had to be poured into slaves and supplies and during that time one could not enjoy what money he made. A career on the river was, it seemed, far more suitable. River life was more in the tempo of his spirit; rivermen did not sit on porches all the time or sweat in cotton fields. They went places and saw things. One failure would not ruin them, for they could start over with only a small initial investment. At a certain time in his life Andrew had listened gravely to people like his father, who called his love of water "boyish fancy." Now he contested their views.

In the responsible job of overseer he was learning to have faith in his own ideas. He knew what he wanted. For the present time, however, he decided to remain as George's overseer. George needed him and he felt a certain responsibility to finish the plans that his brother had asked him to carry out. To discard a position of trust, particularly one which involved someone so close, was against the nature of Andrew Smyth. It was good to be trusted by people even if their gratitude was small. The

[11] Andrew F. Smyth, n. p., to M. C. Smyth, ca. 1840. AFS MSS.
[12] Freund, *Houston Journal,* p. 61.

public respect of a principled man could sometimes be worth more than "the wit of one who is unscrupulous."[13]

An awareness of honesty, vital in the life of old Captain Smyth, had become so much a part of Andrew that he took a special delight in it. While the miller held honesty as a mark of gentility, Andrew liked the idea of it, if only as a way of life, with no reason except the pleasure of being that way, trusted by those who knew him. He was said to be frank in his opinions, correct to the cent in business transactions. This reputation which he had acquired as overseer might be damaged or cut short should he quit the job at a precarious time. It was not easy to build a good name in a new place, where everyone's origins were suspected at first. A respected brother's influence could help, but it could only go so far. Andrew believed that an honorable name, once made, was the enduring step toward a rich future. The Alabama boy had lost no time.

[13] Andrew F. Smyth, fragment of either a letter or an essay, n. d. AFS MSS.

PART TWO

A Multitude of Dreams

5. When it was time to plant the cotton crop of 1844 the planned improvements at George W. Smyth's farm had been made. Andrew, as overseer, could be particularly proud of what three years had accomplished. He had given himself entirely to every facet of the program.

I

The log house had been enlarged with a second floor of finished lumber and with chimneys of brick. A good distance from the residence stood the kitchen and dining room in a separate building, beyond which were the small tannery, sugar house, and slave quarters in one direction, and the main barns and cotton sheds in another. Immediately to the north side of the house was a bridge spanning Walnut Run and giving access to the road to Bevilport and the little town of Pinetuckey. Beside the bridge was the cemetery, enclosed by a picket fence.

The "big house" itself could not have been called elegant in any other setting, but here it might even be called a mansion. Saddles were probably laid at random on the front porch and it is doubtful that anything was painted or even whitewashed. Yet the irregular bigness, coupled with the owners' love of extravagant social graces and consequently the manner in which the house was used, produced a feeling of real luxury. In the flower garden before the house were pine-needle walkways and a brass sundial on a pedestal. George had made this sundial for Frances, and he valued it second only to his library. There were now four children, who with their parents and Andrew managed to crowd even this house.

Things at last had permanence. The wood of the buildings was mellowed in the older sections to form a venerable background for the vines and shrubs, which had advanced enough to shade the house. Drusilla and January's importance and nearness to the family were reflected in the tokens of respect added to their names—Mammy Silla and Uncle January.

Down in Jefferson County, Joseph Grigsby was dead, his effects sold publicly in an effort to settle the estate. Joining the rest of the family at the auction, George had bought three Negroes to add to his holdings at the farm.[1] Sally Grigsby came to live with her daughter, bringing her four house servants and particularly handsome table silver. Her fine house at Grigsby's Bluff was closed and finally divided into apartments for two overseers and their families; unpainted, like George's, that house did not take long to fall into ruin, for the tenants paid little attention to its maintenance.

Andrew enjoyed his association with this pleasant, prosperous family circle. His planting efforts in 1844 were given over entirely to cotton, the money crop.[2]

Andrew was ready now to set out on his own. Although he would continue to live with his brother, he was replaced in the job of overseer by Uncle January, who took up that responsibility after the crop was planted. The population of the county had grown and if the discussed annexation of Texas by the United States really happened, an even greater increase would occur. Stores in Jasper and Bevilport still needed merchandise, just as the farmers wanted assurance that their cotton would get to market. Andrew was as much aware of these needs as anyone, for he had faced the problem of getting three cotton crops to market and had experienced no end of complications.

The rivermen more or less appeared out of nowhere, making the farmers reluctant to trust them with transporting valuable bales of cotton. The cotton in many instances, upon investigation, had been found waterlogged at the bottom of the Neches, near the floating shambles of a wrecked flatboat. In those cases the rivermen had fled the scene unless they had insurance, which they rarely did when the matter was checked into, in spite of what they had said at Bevilport. River hazards were to be expected and honest rivermen faced them, but did not run away in the event of an accident. Unfortunately, not enough honest men were available to answer the need of the area.

At its end the Neches River flowed into Sabine Lake, which was separated from the Gulf of Mexico by a narrow channel, Sabine Pass. Sabine City, also called Sabine Pass, had grown up beside the lake, profiting in part from the trade of the upriver Neches and the Sabine, which also emptied into the lake. Conspicuously new, Sabine Pass had a number of mercantile houses along its streets. These houses could supply most backwoods needs.

[1] Estate of Joseph Grigsby to George W. Smyth, bill of sale for slaves, July 20, 1840. AFS MSS.
[2] Account books of Andrew F. Smyth in connection with the Walnut Run farm, 1842. AFS MSS.

The city of Galveston loomed on its island forty miles westward along the coast from Sabine Pass. Those who wished to reach Galveston from the Pass either went overland or on a schooner or steamboat by way of the choppy Gulf. If a certain article could not be found in the stores of Galveston it could not be found in Texas, for here was the Republic's trade center. Ships arrived daily from New Orleans bringing things to tempt the imaginations of country and city folk alike. Everything from barrels of sugar to Grecian tables was unloaded to be replaced by Texas cotton, hides, and lumber, all headed for the United States. Ships also came from Europe and the West Indies with rich cargoes, although those from the United States were more frequent.

Foreign merchandise was deposited at Sabine Pass in small quantities because only ships of limited size were able to cross the sand bar and dock there.[3] Merchants ordered goods which could be quickly sold to local people or to customers upriver; farmers grew cotton to ship to buyers downriver.

In this seemingly happy transfer a dangerous gap existed keeping merchant and backwoodsmen apart: store goods gathered dust, and cotton ruined in the shed when transportation was not available.[4] A distance of fifty to one hundred miles was an impenetrable wall in such a case, for to depend upon the Republic's poor roads was senseless. Realizing that the water was the cheap and efficient means of transportation, an ambitious man, at very little expense, could fill this gap and reap a profit. The possibility appealed to Andrew and he took steps to secure clients among the farmers.

II

Meanwhile, George and Frances had confronted Andrew with the topic of marriage. A young man with ambition was a sought-after guest in those parts for dances and Sunday meals, specifically where there were eligible daughters in the host's family. If the bachelor himself was not involved in a search for a wife, it was believed that he should at least start thinking along those lines.

Andrew was twenty-seven, was a hard worker, was generally considered levelheaded, and was not given to excessive drinking or gambling. Because there was no Presbyterian congregation, he had begun to at-

---

[3] Willis W. Pratt (ed.), *Galveston Island; or a Few Months off the Coast of Texas: The Journal of Francis C. Sheridan, 1839–1840,* pp. 127–128.

[4] Earl Wesley Fornell, *The Galveston Era: The Texas Crescent on the Eve of Secession,* p. 27.

tend the Baptist church each month, most times in company with his sister-in-law and her children, and as overseer he had seen that the Walnut Run Negroes were well represented in the slave gallery of the meeting house. Indeed, it is remembered that Mammy Silla's rendition of hymns was missed by no one within a half mile of the church, and her zeal was probably considered to be a credit to the overseer. While Andrew's grammar was not the best, he was trained in surveying, which bespoke of an education and could certainly be used, if need be, to supplement an income later on. He had questioned his family in letters as to the welfare of certain young ladies in Moulton, but one by one these girls had married.[5] Because he had been in this part of Texas almost nine years he probably would find his future wife in Jasper County.

Before they were fifteen, single females in this Republic, in this very county, began considering likely mates. In fact, their parents, with perhaps eleven other mouths to feed, might give the matter greater concern. A dress which in some past day had graced a Georgia or South Carolina ballroom, was now altered to fit a Jasper belle. The mother, working with homemade needles, could remember when the gown was new. What if it had become threadbare? At least it was silk and not homespun. But to what rewards had this gown come? It was fortunate if its hem lasted through an evening on puncheon floors, or if its skirt remained intact brushing against log walls. Such things didn't really matter, for the object of it all was that the belle become a bride, and after the dress had served as a wedding gown the mother would pack it away for a little sister, whose time had yet to come. Men far outnumbered women during the days of the Republic, and if a girl escaped the altar it was through a determination on her own part.

No particular girl in Jasper County seems to have appealed to Andrew, nor he to them. George and Frances continually advised their brother of certain girls' good points and at the same time warned him to avoid others, whose parents had, in the early days, visited the priest later than they should have. Frances was articulate on that subject. Andrew was indifferent.

When Joseph Grigsby had moved to Texas from Kentucky he had left behind several married daughters. One of these daughters was Nancy, the wife of Benjamin Allen, a resident of Daviess County, Kentucky. To Nancy and Benjamin six children had been born. The second child was named Emily. At seventeen, in 1844, Emily had been writing her Aunt

5 M. Constantine Smyth, Moulton, Alabama, to Andrew F. Smyth, March 6, 1844. GWS MSS, UTA.

Frances in Texas. The letters were long and involved, for Emily loved to relate family experiences and anecdotes about people that she knew Frances had not seen in many years.

Frances, at home, read the letters aloud for her household to hear. People isolated in the country looked upon letters as exciting forms of amusement to be read, discussed, and reread.

Andrew's enjoyment of the letters of Emily Allen did not pass unnoticed by George and Frances. When they inquired they were told that the letters made Emily sound like a "sensible girl." Of course, Andrew was not going to write to her, nor did he want to be teased just because several letters had entertained him more than they did anyone else. Nonetheless, he managed to collect information on Miss Allen in subtle ways through conversations with Sally Grigsby, her grandmother.

George and Frances, knowing nothing of this, finally gave up their matrimonial campaign in desperation. Andrew had business on his mind and it was apparent that only river talk and flatboats would stir him.

III

During 1844, while Andrew prepared to begin his river enterprise, George was elected to the House of Representatives of the Republic from Jasper County. Sam Houston, nearing the end of his second presidency, had exerted himself in favor of annexation. Revenge-hungry Mexicans, not to mention the Indians and land speculators within Texas, had presented problems to this administration, but the annexation question was given more attention than anything else. American abolitionists spoke loudly against annexation, with an opposition fighting in equal force. In December, Houston would be replaced by Dr. Anson Jones, the newly elected president.

For George, the months in the capital would be exciting and not one minute must be missed. Andrew's plans, for once, were altered little by his brother's absence from the county. He would begin his business and still have time, while at home, to consult with Uncle January about the operation of the Walnut Run farm.

Before the winter rains came, Jasper County farmers saw that their cotton was out of the fields. The cotton was ordinarily stored in large, open-sided sheds built for that purpose. If the farmer did not own a gin —which was usually the case—he loaded his cotton into high-sided wagons and went to the nearest farm that had a gin, where for a fee he could have his cotton processed. Included in the fee was the compressing of the ginned cotton into three- to five-hundred-pound bales. Having bargained with a buyer from Sabine Pass or Galveston, he looked for a means of getting his bales to one of those cities. Here Andrew stepped in.

From the timber on his Angelina River land he had fashioned a flatboat, which was tied up at the Bevilport landing. For one dollar a bale he would transport the cotton safely to Sabine Pass, and, if the client wished, arrangements would be made for shipping it on to Galveston or New Orleans aboard a schooner.[6] The farmers' money would be delivered to them when Andrew was home again.

As overseer and as George's brother, Andrew had made many valuable friends in the county and his reputation as a surveyor had undoubtedly helped him make more. He had all available space on the flatboat reserved even before the boat was built. And he knew that because of the irregular shipping from Bevilport downriver, he could probably be as lucky in getting a full load in any month of the year.

A flatboat in its most elaborate design was a rectangular vessel, resembling a long, shallow box with straight sides and a flat bottom, which sloped up at both ends to the upper rim. The cargo was stacked on the bottom of the boat, protected by the sides and covered with a roof of thick timbers. Andrew's first flatboat was roofless, although a partial wooden covering was built over the cargo to serve as a floor for the tent which he used for living quarters. Strong saplings were cut for poles which would be used to guide the boat.

Floating down the Angelina from Andrew's upriver property, the empty boat was tested under various conditions. At one place Indian Creek poured into the river, creating a whirlpool and currents strong enough to thrust the boat into the bank; also, the rocky shoals just above Bevilport formed a shallow spot difficult to cross. The three helpers who worked with Andrew were either hired outright or were promised part of the profit from the trip.

The four poled the boat to the Bevilport landing and began loading cotton and tobacco aboard. At Bevilport the Angelina was narrow and shaded by trees, which usually allowed only a narrow slice of sunlight on the surface of the river. In this small area were other flatboats, some rafts, and probably a keelboat or two. The cotton bales were stacked closely in rows one on top of another. After the loading was completed came the problem of getting the mass of boats moved around so that the channel was cleared for those who wished to leave. Even with such

---

[6] Andrew F. Smyth account book, 1844. AFS MSS.

crowded conditions at the dock, shipping was so inadequate that some farmers had to travel to the Sabine in hopes of engaging a flatboat there.

From the Angelina the flatboat was poled into the current of the Neches. Andrew and the men with him took turns with the poles, pushing the boat away from the riverbanks each time it tended toward one or the other. A person could not possibly man a flatboat alone, for constant attention was required—here a treacherous snag threatened to rip the side of the boat, there a shallow area demanded a quick-witted touch with the poles. A real riverman handled his pole with an almost artistic grace, avoiding dangerous places expertly with no damage to the boat or the cargo.

The water varied from muddy brown upriver to black toward the coast. At no place could the bottom of the river be viewed. The current was continuous but gradual and at the edges of the river the water was still, reflecting walls of trees. The only noise was that made by the boat. Alligators and moccasins had to be watched for, even if they seemed harmless compared to low-hanging limbs and submerged trees.

At night the boat was tied to the riverbank, as the men alternately slept and kept watch. Andrew carried the rifle that old Captain Smyth had bought for him years before, in April, after a particularly prosperous season at the gristmill. No riverman or land traveler was wise to journey in the isolated parts of the Republic unarmed; this section was dangerous because desperadoes from the United States, crossing the Sabine, sometimes came here on their way to Mexico or to other parts of Texas. Besides having criminals to worry about, the crew had to be on the alert for snakes, wildcats, and bears. In the daytime, when no obstructions were evident in the river, all on board could relax. But these times were few. The Neches River had never been improved for navigation and every bend that it took was almost certain to harbor danger of some kind.

Riding the current finally into Sabine Lake, the flatboat was towed across to Sabine Pass by a steamer which performed that service for a small charge.[7] About a month had gone by since the flatboat left Bevilport.

In Sabine Pass, warehouse space was found for the cotton, or schooner passage to Galveston or New Orleans was arranged for it. Andrew went to the office of the cotton buyer and was paid in gold for the cargo. Because a growing town like Sabine Pass needed lumber for its new build-

[7] *Ibid.*

ings he had no trouble selling the flatboat for the materials used in its construction. The profit from the sale of the flatboat was equal to that made from transporting cotton, if not greater.

The expenses of the trip, except for the food and salaries of the other rivermen, came from the farmers' cotton money. After the warehouse proprietor and the schooner captain and the steamboat captain had been paid, the cotton money was put in a money belt and Andrew rode horseback home to Jasper County. Flatboats could not make the trip upriver. The journey would be difficult and foolish as well, considering that it was simpler to build a new boat than to bother with the old one. At Bevilport, where he met his clients, all accounts were settled in cash, on the spot.

Andrew wanted to build a keelboat eventually. A keelboat could fight the current and bring goods upriver from the coast. But a keelboat was a fine vessel and not one which could be hurriedly built. Until he was financially ahead, therefore, a one-way flatboat business would have to do. When money was more plentiful, business would indeed be extended.

Andrew's Angelina River land was situated at an inconvenient distance from Bevilport, and the shoals in the river made it inaccessible during times of low water. Aware of the advantages of river land near the economic center of the county, he began to inquire about available property.

An undivided 1,060 acres a mile or so upriver from Bevilport's landing seemed the ideal place. The land was owned by R. C. Doom, a Bevilport merchant, and James Carr Everitt, son of the late Dr. Everitt. Although the owners were willing to sell, the title to the acreage was unclear, owing to difficulties which had arisen in the settlement of Dr. Everitt's estate. Early in 1845 Doom and Everitt requested that the county probate court appoint commissioners to divide the land. After the commissioners' report was submitted the sale of the land would be discussed with Andrew.

George, an authority on land titles, advised Andrew in the matter. The price that the owners decided upon was not out of reason, but it was more than Andrew could pay. Since the land was so perfectly suited to Andrew's needs George suggested that some arrangements be made for buying it over a period of time and that Andrew begin transactions as soon as possible.[8]

[8] Abstract of the William Jordan Survey, Jasper County, Texas, that part which contains the 1,060 acres which Andrew was interested in; George W. Smyth, Galveston, Texas, to Andrew F. Smyth, January 7, 1845. AFS MSS.

While this discussion was still in progress Andrew built another flat-boat. By the last week in April he was in Sabine Pass again, but this time he would not return upriver right away. If he had advised George and Frances of his plans in advance, they were perhaps a bit dumb-founded yet. Settling his affairs at the Pass, he prepared to leave for Kentucky, where he would introduce himself to Emily Allen.

IV

The fastest way to reach the main parts of the United States from the Republic of Texas was by sea. Andrew went to Galveston from Sabine Pass and bought a ticket on a steamer bound for New Orleans. He was in Galveston four days waiting for the boat to leave. Arranging for ac-commodations in a boarding house, he set out to see the sights of Gal-veston and particularly the stores, which held a notorious fascination for country people.

With money that he had made from the two flatboats he was anxious to replace his homespun clothes with some more suited to a man of the world. Each of his purchases was recorded in the small blue account book which he carried in his pocket. The entries in this book were neat and written with attention to clarity; it was hard to believe that the author of the cluttered letters and the keeper of this book were the same man.

Somewhere in the city he bought a broadcloth suit, a satin vest, and a silk cravat. He touched all this sumptuousness off with a diamond stickpin in the shape of an S.[9] Each item was paid for in cash.

For the duration of his stay on the island, he found several interesting things that he could do to occupy his time. He took great pleasure in watching the ships enter the port, cumbersome creaking sailing ships or sleek steamers, their curiously dressed sailors unloading goods for the great mercantile houses. And in the saloons and restaurants Andrew's new clothes made him feel less like a bumpkin than he had when he first entered the city. For all practical purposes he looked like a prosperous businessman and he hoped that the Allens would take note of that.

After the four days had passed he boarded the steamer *New York* and in a matter of six more days was in New Orleans. He spent some time there, the only modern city which he had seen since he passed through Natchez long ago, at the time of the Revolution. On the waterfront

[9] Andrew F. Smyth account book, 1844. AFS MSS.

Andrew could view more flatboats in one place than existed in the whole Republic of Texas, not to mention the steamboats, some of which were decorated with ornate woodcarvings. Perhaps Andrew wondered if someday regular steamers would ply the Neches and Angelina; he knew that there was already talk in Sabine Pass of starting a packet to Town Bluff every other month.[10]

New Orleans had things to tempt all tastes and the merchandise there, when out of style, was known to find its way to Texas stores, where people knew no better than to buy it. Andrew's Galveston finery had probably seen New Orleans before. Its wearer, seeming not to mind at all, sat for a daguerreotype in the city, proudly clutching his left lapel and poorly concealing the laughter which, for some reason, seems to have nearly overcome him.

The finished picture revealed a young man who had become very sure of himself, a young man who enjoyed life. Had it not been for the hand which he so carefully placed on his lapel, in the center of the picture, one might have believed him to be the carefree son of one of the Louisiana sugar planters. Andrew's hands, however, were the hands of a man who had done hard work.

Early in May he traveled up the Mississippi aboard the riverboat *Yazoo* as far as Cairo, Illinois, where he bought passage on a steamer bound up the Ohio River. At Owensboro, Kentucky, he docked and hired a horse for the six-mile trip along the river to the farmhouse of Benjamin Allen. Soon enough he stood before Emily Allen.

Emily was eighteen and had lived in this modest clapboard house all her life. Her father was not a rich man, but his wife, Nancy, had a certain lavish way of doing things that gave guests a pampered feeling. About their home was an air of niceness. The few slaves were well clothed and fed and the fields of cotton and tobacco evidenced that Benjamin spent little time resting on the porch.

Emily was not as pretty as her Aunt Frances, though the strength of her small, sharp features was vaguely reminiscent of the wife of George W. Smyth. She had to look up to Andrew's face, for she was not over five feet tall; her dark, thin hair accentuated deep-set eyes and white skin, which had been inconsistently protected from the sun. To Andrew, her small hands seemed not so well accustomed to domestic work as they

---

[10] Andrew F. Smyth, New Orleans, Louisiana, to George W. Smyth, May 16, 1844. AFS MSS.

were. He liked the style of this country girl, who had never been beyond Daviess County, Kentucky.[11]

Andrew remained at the Allens' home for several weeks, speaking often, no doubt, of Texas and flatboats, of the fine Walnut Run farm, and of the county of Jasper, in which it stood. In her correspondence with her sister, Nancy Allen had learned of Andrew's success as overseer of the farm. The Allens and their friends were curious as to what it was like to live in the Republic that might someday be a state in the Union.

And as far as Emily was concerned, Andrew seems to have been fascinated. She was a little shy, like him, just enough to make him speak out and say things. There were no silly notions in her head; she did not wish to see the world, at least at the moment, for she was sincerely interested in the responsibilities which her life had already given her.

Andrew and Emily enjoyed being together during the weeks of June. When the time came for Andrew to leave he proposed marriage to her. If the proposal seemed abrupt to her parents, they might be reminded that Texas was a long way from Kentucky, meaning that a rejection on their part would undoubtedly end Andrew and Emily's chances of even seeing one another again. They were fond of Andrew and since Emily wanted them to agree they made preparations for a wedding.[12] The marriage took place in midsummer at the Allens' home.

Before the newlyweds left the Allen farm, a young slave girl, Ann, cried that she wanted to go with Miss Emily. Moved by this request, Benjamin Allen transferred ownership of the girl to his daughter, along with a cow, a horse, and a mule. Nancy filled a trunk with bolts of cloth, a few nice china plates, and a silver tea service.

During August, Andrew and Emily bid the Allens farewell and began their overland journey. In Alabama they spent a week with Captain Smyth at the mill, leaving the old man in good spirits, again thinking that he should move to Texas. In every condition of land and weather the little party traveled—Emily and Ann on the mule and Andrew on the horse, leading a pack horse and the cow. They moved through rainy forests and busy towns, beside wild rivers and still ponds, until the beginning of October, when they crossed the Sabine into Texas.

[11] Nancy Allen, Daviess County, Kentucky, to Emily Allen Smyth, 1848. AFS MSS.
[12] *Ibid.*

6. Frances was alone when Andrew and Emily arrived at the Walnut Run place in the fall. George, having been home from the capital only a short time, was recalled in June to a special session of Congress.[1] As everyone knew, the topic of discussion was annexation.

I

The Congress of the Republic had, in its regular session, offered Texas for annexation by the United States; the United States, however, had opposition to this in its own Congress, as evidenced by Henry Clay's and Martin Van Buren's rejection of the proposal. Clay was the Whig candidate for president and Van Buren, it was believed, would have the Democratic nomination. Sam Houston and President Anson Jones then embarked upon a program of conspicuous friendliness toward Great Britain and France, in an effort, it is believed, to bring matters to a climax. Faced with the prospect of Texas joining one of the European powers and withdrawing the offer of annexation from the United States entirely, American sentiment swayed. In fact, it changed so radically that James K. Polk, in favor of annexing Texas, won the Democratic nomination and eventually the presidency. Meanwhile, Mexico, under a new leader, proposed to recognize Texas' independence, provided that the idea of annexation to the United States be dropped—forever. To the men who wanted the Republic to live on, this was appealing. When on March 1, 1845, the American Congress passed a resolution inviting Texas to join the Union, Anson Jones called a June meeting of the Congress of the Republic. George, of course, was there. The Mexican proposal was presented, along with that of the United States. Congress voted in favor of the latter, as did the people of the Republic in a general election.

The people were directed to elect delegates to a convention which would write the state constitution. George was sent from Jasper County and that is where he was when Andrew and Emily arrived from Kentucky.[2]

[1] Winnie Allen (ed.), "The Autobiography of George W. Smith," *Southwestern Historical Quarterly*, XXXVI (January 1933), 213.
[2] *Ibid.*

Because Emily had been about one year old when the Grigsbys left for Texas she and Frances had known each other only through letters. There was much that Emily could ask her aunt concerning Texas life. Both Frances and Sally Grigsby were capable of performing the various tasks that fell upon country women, even those with slaves. In the past Emily had assumed some of the domestic duties which would ordinarily have been attended to by her mother, but her work had always been planned for her by Nancy. Never had she managed a household on her own.

Until they had established themselves, the young Smyths would live at Walnut Run and although Andrew could not hope soon to build so fine a place for Emily, she would have the opportunity during this short visit with Frances and Sally to learn about the setting up and maintenance of an East Texas home.[3] In October or early November, Emily announced that she was pregnant.

Andrew was advised that the commissioners selected by R. C. Doom and James Carr Everitt had come to a decision. The 1,060 acres near Bevilport would be "injured in point of value" by a division. The probate court said that the land would be sold at public auction for no less than two thirds of its appraised value, which would be $530.[4] Andrew did not have the money, nor did he wish to take a risk by agreeing to pay on a twelve-months' credit arrangement.

Whether he could afford it or not, he wanted the land. Years before, when land was plentiful, he might have withdrawn from the matter altogether, because other good locations would be available; now, however, he had Emily as well as himself to consider and this river property was too advantageous a purchase to pass up. Somehow he did not want his brother's assistance.[5]

Riding to R. C. Doom's farm east of Bevilport, Andrew confronted him with the problem. Mr. Doom was willing to arrange for a loan, but he required mortgages on Andrew's land. This decision brought things to a standstill, for land grants issued by the Republic could not be mortgaged or sold. The law had originated as an effort to curb speculation in land.

Andrew's problem was brought to the attention of Patrick Hussey,

[3] Andrew and Emily's mail was at this time addressed in care of George W. Smyth, Walnut Run, Jasper County, Texas.
[4] Abstract of the William Jordan Survey, Jasper County, Texas. AFS MSS.
[5] George W. Smyth, Texas, to Andrew F. Smyth, November 20, 1845. AFS MSS.

who had been a neighbor back in Moulton and was now a farmer in Jasper County. Patrick said that he would buy the land, with Doom's backing, for Andrew. Andrew would be allowed to use the land and when he was able to buy it the market price, counting the improvements, would be asked. In this manner Patrick stood a chance of making a profit, seeing that Texas land, now safely in the United States, would likely rise in value.

As scheduled, the auction took place in Jasper on the courthouse square the second Tuesday in December. Patrick bid $530 and the land was his on paper, Andrew's by virtue of a gentlemen's agreement. Better land deals had been made, to be sure. But Andrew had enough faith in this investment to be quite confident that he would have no difficulty in eventually paying for it.

James K. Polk, on December 29, 1845, signed the bill admitting Texas into the United States. The terms of annexation had been drawn up at a July meeting of the Congress of the Republic: Texas would be admitted at once as a state, not having to become a territory first; Texas would pay her own debts but could dispose of the public lands as she pleased; and if Texas was divided into smaller states, some of the new states would be nonslaveholding.

George W. Smyth was among the men who wrote the state constitution, which fulfilled the requirements imposed by the United States.

To many, annexation meant the death of a potentially great country. Winning independence had not been easy. It had been a game of chance which had brought pride and optimism to men who had not experienced nation-making before. In many minds was an unspoken reluctance about being American again, although the same minds would relax, knowing that the gamble was at an end. Where a few dreamers had envisioned the fantastic, the majority had lived from day to day, like Andrew, solving problems as they came, working to reap the good life from this land.

Andrew and Emily were moving into their new home in February, 1846, when Anson Jones, in a ceremony miles away, ended forever the Republic of Texas.

II

Andrew must have been anxious to complete his house and turn to his business, for the cabin was ready by the end of winter. His 1,060 acres extended for several miles along the narrow, muddy Angelina. Covered

1. The Andrew Smyth residence. "Emily's new house," as it appeared in 1957, in disrepair. The chimney on the ell was gone, as were the many outbuildings. Photograph by Jack B. Osborne.

2. Emily Allen Smyth, pictured in Owensboro, Kentucky, by a traveling daguerreotypist shortly before her marriage to Andrew. AFS MSS.

3. Captain Andrew Smyth, in New Orleans, while on his way to Kentucky to meet Emily in 1845.   AFS MSS.

4. George W. Smyth at the time when he was land commissioner for the state of Texas (c. 1848–1857). AFS MSS.

5. Colonel P. F. Renfro, an investor in the *Laura*. Courtesy of Gertrude Seale Appling.

6. The *Laura*, circa 1878. This photograph was circulated along the Neches and Angelina Rivers as advertisement for a Galveston photographer. AFS MSS.

7. Captain Kellie's Jefferson Rifles marching in Jasper in the 1870's. Veterans of the Texas Revolution and the Mexican War did not walk, but were allowed to ride in the buggies.   Courtesy of Mrs. Arthur Few.

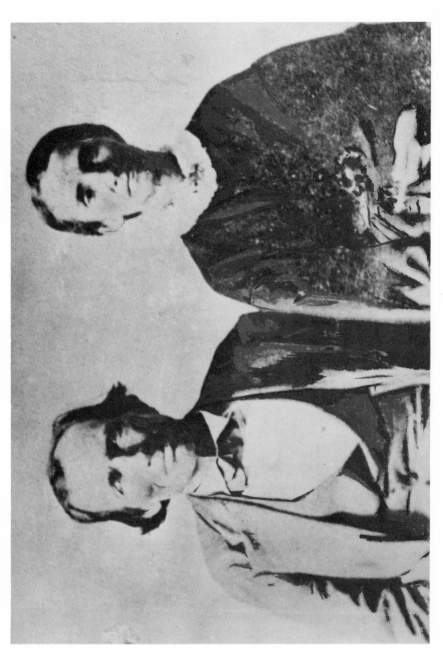

8. Andrew and Emily Smyth pictured in Galveston in 1878. AFS MSS.

by dark woods up to the river's edge, the land tilted upward for a distance inland to what Andrew considered the back of his property. Along the riverbank the soil was rich and black, good for planting, while that of the backland was sandy, useful mainly for the trees which covered it. All Jasper County's trees were represented here in a continuous forest, which apparently had never been entered by a woodsman. The pine needles and leaves of many years lay in layers on the ground, creating a moist place where ferns grew. Even in the sandy backland, wet-weather creeks held rainwater so that it could soak into the soil and not drain into the swamp or the river, as it would ordinarily have done. Cane thrived at the edge of the big swamp, located a short distance from the riverbank, and in this swamp were the ancient cypress trees which Andrew considered one of the major advantages of his purchase. Although lower than most, the land was like the other parts of Jasper County.

A good distance before it poured into the river, Indian Creek passed through Andrew's property, giving a dependable supply of good water. At its end the water gashed deeply through the riverbank and on one of the steep slopes which it left at the mouth of the creek, Andrew built his cabin.

The house was certainly of the rudest sort, having only one room downstairs and a loft to accommodate Ann. If there was a chimney it was of mud and sticks as the first ones at Walnut Run had been. From any place near the cabin, or within, the sound of running water could be heard; the door was not a great distance from the chasm where the creek joined the river and created a noisy whirlpool, in whose waters were captured tree limbs and pine cones and other forest things which the currents of both streams brought there.

Andrew liked being near the water but Emily expressed her misgivings at the location, saying that the convenience and beauty of the site were no compensation for the danger involved. Her pregnancy seems not to have interfered with her determination to make a pleasant home for her husband. And Andrew returned to his business as soon as he and Emily had moved from the Walnut Run farm.

It excited them to reach for better things, realizing full well that they had little to start with and that ahead were months and years of work to be done.

III

The new location simplified Andrew's flatboat enterprise in that he was nearer Bevilport. To build a flatboat, no longer would he have to stay far upriver in the loneliness of a camp with only his few employees to keep him company. Now he could go to town in a skiff, transact business, return home, and still have a half day left, during which he could work on the boat.

He could eat his meals at the table with his wife and enjoy hearing her make declarations and domestic complaints about the difficulties of women in the country; they had time now to discuss what they would name their child and what store-bought things Andrew needed to get with the profit of his next trip downriver. The stay at Walnut Run for Emily had been an interim in her marriage before she could set in operation a home of her own. For Andrew, knowing that his business could be attended to, right in the midst of the pleasures of home, was pure delight.

Since building a flatboat was no easy task, for assistance Andrew hired four "Congo Negroes" from a farmer in the county. Used to heavy work with the axe, these men squared logs and fashioned flatboats in less time than it had taken Andrew with two workers or partners on past projects.[6] The flatboat was usually built on the riverbank at the shoals. A space had been cleared there where the logs from the woods could be stacked and adapted with the axe to fill a particular need in the structure of the flatboat. In stripping the bark away from the logs, the Negroes handled machettes with such frequency and roughness that hereafter Andrew had to buy new knives on each trip downriver. The Negroes worked fast and well, and soon Andrew had trained them to act as crewmen on the ride to the Gulf.[7]

After three or so weeks of working constantly, smelling fluid sap and raw cut wood, and striving to bind and peg the boat together, Andrew and the Negroes slid the vessel down into the current to Bevilport, where farmers had been arriving for days with wagonloads of cotton. Andrew took three flatboats to Sabine Pass in the spring of 1846. The cargo of each of the boats was primarily cotton, with a shipment of tobacco carried on the third. The freight rate for cotton was still one dollar per bale and on his April trip, which was representative, ninety-four bales were transported, the expense to Andrew amounting to ten dollars.[8]

Before the flatboat left Bevilport, people approached Andrew with

[6] Andrew F. Smyth account book, 1946. AFS MSS.
[7] *Ibid.*
[8] *Ibid.*

lists of goods they needed from Sabine Pass or Galveston. Andrew, as a favor, took the lists to various merchants, bought and paid for the goods, and scheduled a place for the purchases on the next boat upriver.[9] On at least two of his trips he brought packhorses from Sabine Pass to Bevilport, carrying various items that he had bought for people. But these ventures had been more trouble than they were worth, for they delayed beginning another flatboat by one week, and he found that he was exhausted by the time he reached home. Since he had first known the transportation business in the backwoods, Andrew had realized the value of keelboats, for, other than steamboats, they were the only means of fighting the current of the river.

Keelboats were sturdy and had no machinery to bother with. It had been said, and perhaps with some wisdom, that steamboats would never bother with the unimproved waters of the Angelina and the Neches; indeed, the first of many steamers had traveled the Sabine in 1839, and though the river needed few improvements in the first place, the captains complained that it was a hazardous journey to make.[10] The apparent foolishness of taking greater chances on the Neches was probably the reason that talk of a regular packet every other month to Town Bluff had died out.

With a keelboat one did not have as many reasons to worry about dangers. A keelboat itself reminded one of a compact Noah's Ark, which would be difficult to damage, even in the event of a rough river, snags, or low-hanging timber at the river's edge. Depending entirely upon the current for power, it needed no store of fuel nor any metal parts, impossible to obtain in an upriver place like Bevilport.

Andrew knew that if it was worth his time to take cotton to market, he could count upon even better profits from bringing store-bought things back to the farmers. This keelboat business had been tried before by rivermen of the seasoned sort, who did not work when they were money ahead but went into merry retirement at the end of each voyage until their cash was gone and they had borrowed all that they could. Consequently, no one could depend upon the keelboatmen, and some farmers went to the extreme of building their own keelboats, as had R. C. Doom, several years before he sold Andrew the river land. As Andrew planned to expand his river career, he realized that public trust was

---

[9] *The Beaumont Journal,* Beaumont, Texas, September 12, 1925, Sec. 2, p. 1 (clipping).
[10] "Texas Cotton," Ben Stuart MS, p. 5.

70 TEXAS RIVERMAN

one of the foundation stones of success.[11] Sometime before summer, 1846, he decided to build a keelboat.

A keelboat was more expertly designed than a flatboat and required a great deal more work to build. Before beginning construction Andrew planned his boat on paper. In floorplan it was a long, narrow oval, pointed at both ends. The boat had space for a roomy hold and a small cabin, which was above the level of the deck.[12] An enormous rudder, turned by a long, bent pole, perched comically at one end of the boat and could be transferred to the opposite place if the boat needed to go in the other direction. With the rudder and the sharp bow the current could be sliced more successfully than it had been with the blunt nose of the flatboat. The cabin, though small, was a great improvement over the tent which had been used on the flatboat. There was a table, a hearth located beneath an opening in the roof, and a bunk or two attached to the walls. The odd-shaped windows had wooden shutters but no glass, through which the shafts of light would be diffused into the cramped gloom of the cabin.

Within the cabin and upon its roof would be the only floored spaces where Andrew, his crew, or the occasional passenger might remain at leisure. The remainder of the boat would, when business was good, be packed with cotton bales or goods from the mercantile houses downriver. Andrew's boat probably did not have sails, for the narrow channels which the river made through the woods permitted little wind. Once he had designed his boat, he and his employees set to work on it.

To his list of four Negro helpers Andrew added a white man named Holland. Lumber was cut from logs which had been dragged to the spot set aside for building. Representing weeks of sawing and bending timbers, the finished boat had gradually rounded sides, flat decks, and an arched roof.[13]

The boat was tied at the Bevilport landing June 7, and her owner named her the *Jasper*.[14] Bevilport was her home port, a fact noticed by local people with some interest. She had appeared from nowhere. Those who had talked to Andrew supposed that he had worked for the entire past month, giving attention to nothing but his keelboat. They were correct. He had labored long and hard, by torchlight and during

[11] Andrew F. Smyth, Jasper County, Texas, to Captain Andrew Smyth, 1846. AFS MSS.
[12] Sketch plan of the keelboat *Jasper*, marked "A. F. S., 1846." AFS MSS.
[13] Account book for the keelboat, *Jasper*, 1846. AFS MSS.
[14] *Ibid.*

the day. His tools had lain idle only once and that was in May when Emily gave birth to a daughter at the cabin on Indian Creek.

On the June trip to Sabine Pass, Andrew took a flatboat as well as the new keelboat.[15] Although the two boats probably moved at a fairly even rate, the keelboat was pure luxury to handle compared to its lumbering companion. The swift current was at the center of the river and if the keelboat needed to be slowed down, a slight turn of the rudder directed it to the calm, gradual waters near the shore. Poles were used only in hazardous places.

To man the flatboat were three Negroes, while Andrew, Holland, and the fourth Negro operated the *Jasper*.[16] As they stopped at plantation landings like George's at the mouth of Walnut Run, or at villages like Town Bluff, additional cotton was stacked onto the cargo already loaded at Bevilport. With few exceptions the loads were accompanied by lists of goods to be bought at the coast. Most of the trip required merely a lazy watchfulness at the rudder, for the river kept the boat in motion. There was no reason not to relax, and space to nap could be found among the cotton bales when the weather was good, or in the cabin. The hold and most of the deck were taken up by this largest shipment of cotton which Andrew had ever handled.

In Sabine Pass the flatboat was emptied and sold for a price high enough to indicate that Andrew had used as much lumber in its construction as he could. Again, the profit from the sale of the flatboat exceeded that from the shipping of the cargo. Money was to be made from upriver timber. Andrew took note of this on more than one occasion and showed a marked interest in the possibility of someday organizing a lumber enterprise. After the cotton was safely stored in one of several warehouses at the Pass, the *Jasper* was tied to the dock and put under guard, so that her master could attend to the remainder of his business.

Having received payment in cash, usually gold, for the farmers' cotton, he could see to filling their orders for store-bought goods. In the homemade account book marked "Andrew F. Smyth, Master, the Jasper," he recorded the number of bales that each farmer had entrusted to him, the market price of the bales, and the various expenses of shipping and buying items at the mercantile houses.

Most of the merchandise lists were long, including every imaginable product from pins to plows. Even Emily had provided him with a list. While the average needs of the backwoodsmen were available in Sabine

[15] *Ibid.*; business papers, June, 1846. AFS MSS.
[16] *Ibid.*

Pass, Andrew sometimes found it necessary to go to Galveston to buy things. Such a trip was required on the maiden voyage of the *Jasper* in 1846. Taking the beach coach at the Pass, Andrew traveled for two days down the barren, sandy peninsula, and was ferried across the bay to Galveston Island in the evening of the second day. There during the next morning he bought and paid for whatever he needed at a big house like Baker and Lusk, and booked passage for himself and the goods aboard the sailing ship *Fairy*, bound for the Pass. At the port of Sabine Pass the merchandise was transferred from the *Fairy* to the *Jasper*. If he had bought supplies for the keelboat, Andrew was ready to begin the harrowing journey upriver.

Once the keelboat had been towed by a steamer to the mouth of the Neches, Andrew had two means of fighting the current. Where the river did not run through thick woods, four or so of the six men went ashore and pulled the boat at the end of a long rope. Poles were used when this towing method was not possible, keeping the keelboat always as close to the river-bank as safety would permit, in an effort to avoid the current. To keep from losing feet—or even miles—one man remained on shore when the boat was poled, keeping a rope taunt between the vessel and a tree. One slip or misuse of the poles might send the boat spinning in the current and in short moments undo an entire day's work. Without the pointed bow, the upriver progress would have been impossible under normal conditions of the water. At night the keelboat was tied to the riverbank and the rivermen slept, after cooking and eating a supper of the plainest sort.[17] Early the next morning another day of sweat and hard, sluggish work began and it is entirely conceivable that the man whose turn it had been to stand watch all night had no time to sleep during the day. No phase of this work was easy, but it was not expected to be so.

In spite of the strenuous labor, rivermen created an enjoyable atmosphere for themselves. And their amusements, like their occupation, were hard. Turned loose in the saloons and brothels of Galveston, rivermen were generally rough customers but only slightly more so than cowmen, runaway youths, and even the occasional farmer, who forgot his dignity and family in the city. The rivermen had no reason for gaining special notoriety for rowdy conduct in port, for the loud places along the waterfronts were patronized by many kinds of people, all of them there for a certain flavor of fun.

17 Grocery orders in the account book for the keelboat *Jasper*, 1846. AFS MSS.

Some rivermen, like Andrew, considered themselves businessmen and were aware of the responsibilities which they held. Though they doubtless tried everything early in their careers and drank and gambled with the best, they reached a point where they wanted to conserve their money and strength for more important matters. These men, then, were moderate in their approach to the wilder and more expensive aspects of river life. When they could, they preferred to associate with ship captains and other men of position, who might help them in some way. Nonetheless, they were rivermen. Their blood flowed at the tempo of the tough lives that they led.

It was on the water that the riverman's world came to be and rarely did he fail to take part in it. Since any physical power that they could muster was needed for work, that which amused them came in the form of words. They spoke a language all their own—richly profane, boastful, and filled with lurid, detailed descriptions—yelling from flatboat to keelboat to steamer in a mock seriousness which was humorous in its burlesque of the surroundings.

To amuse a crew involved in a difficult or dull task, the man at the rudder of the *Jasper* might create a song from the end of his tongue and sing until he was tired, whereupon Andrew or Holland or one of the Negroes would take up the tune and add verses to complicate the story. A salty tale was welcomed with equal enthusiasm. Practical jokes were eternally played, usually with a bit of cruelty.

Amused by a local river ballad which he heard sung, Andrew penciled the words on the back of his account book:[18]

1st—My friend has been the cause of a great separation
    Concerning the part of a favorite one
    Besides the vexation and a great tribulation
    And they-l all be sorry for what they have done

2nd—Farewell to East Texas I am bound for to leave you
    My fortune to try in some foreign land
    My bottles my glasses to my greatest pleasure
    And when we do meet we will join hand in hand.

3rd—I'll drink and be jolly and as melancholly
    I will drownd it away in a bottle of wine
    I'll drownd it away in a full flowing gourd
    And play on the fiddle to pass away time

[18] Account book for the keelboat *Jasper,* 1846. AFS MSS.

4th—There is gold they do say in the rest of our country
    And money is a thing that ladies adore
    I have money enough to bear my life
    And when it is gone I know how to get more.

5th—So fare well to my friends and kind old neighbors
    Like wise to the girl I never more shall see
    This world it is wide and I'll spend it in pleasure
    And I don't care for no one who don't care for me.

6th—When deathe comes for me I'll freely go with him
    I'll pay my last tax and go with him without scorn
    No wife to weep for me no children to suffer
    No one left behind but my friends for to mourn.

7th—I'll be honest and just in all my transactions
    What ear I do promise it all shall be so
    And here is a health to all sound hearted ladies
    For it is hard to find one that is constant as snow.

The river world of the Neches and the Angelina was small. Few vessels plied these rivers and when the *Jasper,* on its hard upriver trip, happened to pass another boat, the crews would stop and talk, delighted at the uncommon opportunity to be with other people. If a barrel of whiskey was along, as it nearly always was, departure from a visit might be delayed until the next day at dawn. At these times the Negroes were given a ration of whiskey and allowed to go a short distance away and amuse themselves as they pleased. Because small towns and plantations along the river frowned upon waterfront merriment of any sort, for obvious reasons, the rivermen enjoyed meeting one another on the water in the countryside. They camped those nights around a fire on the land and drank, talked, and made noise to combat, if in vain, the fantastic loneliness of the woods.

The *Jasper* approached and passed river landings, one, then another, stopping here or there to unload and pay a client, then inched closer to Bevilport. In time she came to the fork where the Angelina entered the Neches. Home was not far away.

The farmers who did not have landings on the river met Andrew at Bevilport to collect their cotton money and store-bought goods.[19] Towns-people collected at the wharf to see what was aboard, while Andrew went to a quiet place to settle his accounts. For Nathaniel Allen, a certain amount in cash, less the cost of freight, the cost of four sacks of salt, a

---

[19] Receipts for keelboat *Jasper* from various cotton farmers 1846–1849. AFS MSS.

portion of the cost of the trip from Sabine Pass to Galveston to purchase a bellows, and the cost of hauling the salt and the bellows aboard the *Jasper* to Bevilport; for Daniel Gallaway, a certain amount in cash, less the cost of freight, the cost of a blanket, flour, coffee, less the cost of transportation. And so forth. The Negroes' master and Holland were paid after Andrew's other accounts had been settled. Reservations were already being made for the next trip; if the river got any lower, however, the trip would have to be postponed. For the present time Andrew would go to his cabin on Indian Creek, there to be with Emily and his daughter and to prepare to go again downriver.

IV

From the mature neatness of the Walnut Run farm Emily had been taken to the cabin beside Indian Creek and the river. Of this unpromising place she was to make a home. At first, it was dreary and terrible to her, the way that the tall forest trees pressed in winter gray at the perimeter of the yard and lots, seeming to yearn for spring when the free flow of their sap would give them the strength to reclaim what Andrew Smyth and his axe had taken away. Emily feared the whirlpool of mingling waters in sight of her door and the animals of the woods that wandered now and again into the clearing.

But to remain was an unspoken command from which she could not run; it was a command which she sensed within herself, for George and Frances and Andrew had pleaded with her to stay at Walnut Run at least until the baby was born.[20] It had been Emily who loaded her trunk and Ann on the mule and had led the mule and her cow to the new cabin on the creek. Andrew followed the procession, happily, to be sure, but amazed at the spunk of the Kentucky girl. Then, feeling confident that his wife could manage the household, even though she was pregnant, Andrew returned to his river business.

If Andrew had faith in Emily's domestic accomplishments, Frances was uncertain. As perfectly as a seasoned actor on a stage, Frances, at the right times, made her entrance into the clearing with Mammy Silla and brimming baskets of food and supplies. She was just about as convincing as an actor. Emily confessed in later years that had it not been for these visits, inexperience and the pressures of the hard life would have caused her to allow her duties to get the best of her.

[20] George W. Smyth, Walnut Run, Jasper County, Texas, to Andrew F. Smyth, January 3, 1846. AFS MSS.

Having made the brief pretenses of a social call, Frances and Mammy Silla slid down from their mules and set to work. All day they sawed, swept, and instructed Emily in matters which they thought deserved attention. When time came to leave, Frances mounted her sidesaddle and looked as though she had spent the afternoon at tea.

Emily admired the way that her aunt could toil long hours and emerge relaxed and beautiful, her head and shoulders draped in the lace mantilla which she always wore away from home, and her hands soft and white. It was with great effort that Emily stayed proper looking at all, for the breezes played tricks with her hair, while the sun never gave her skin a chance to be lovely. Instead of a mantilla she wore a bonnet, reaching a compromise with the sun, and her dresses were tidy but plain. The two women felt their kinship strongly, though in appearance they were very different. Frances departed each time promising to come again for longer visits as the month of the child's birth drew near. And by dark, the niece was left in the clearing with Ann, ready for the work that tomorrow would bring.

Emily had an advantage over most women of the district in that she had a slave. Ann was only a child, but even a child's help was welcomed. Her mother had belonged to Benjamin Allen and had died, leaving five small children, whom the Allens had reared. From the start, Emily had taken a particular interest in this little girl; that fact was one of the reasons why Ann's request had been granted, permitting her to accompany her mistress to Texas.[21]

One of the first projects at the cabin was clearing the brambles and roots from the yard to packing the dirt and sweeping the ground so that snakes could be readily seen around the house. A vegetable garden was planted in March, with undoubtedly some rows of cotton for home use. Frances provided sprigs and seeds from the Walnut Run farm to give Emily a start, at least once sending three Negro men to plow and weed.

As the months passed, Emily was able to do less and less. So long as Andrew was at home, getting assistance on any project was not a problem. But Andrew and his helpers were gone most of the time. To conserve her strength Emily started nothing new after Andrew returned from his April trip downriver. By that time the cabin beside the creek and the river had a settled look. The horse, the cow, and the mule of the Kentucky dowry foraged in fenced lots among the few chickens which Frances had brought. The fact that Ann could ride the horse, instead

---

[21] The United States census of 1850 gives Ann's age as twelve.

of a dangerous skiff, into Bevilport and be back in three hours was a comfort to her mistress, who thus felt not quite so isolated. Around the cabin the earth was well packed, the trees all cut down. Emily had reached a point where she could afford to limit her activities.

Within the cabin, however, were the ever-present duties of cooking and cleaning, neither one overpowering in such a small household. Because log cabin was not impervious to insects, each day it needed to be checked from floor to roof for unwelcome wildlife. Tables, benches, and beds built from saplings or split logs were scrubbed clean and smooth with sand. Spanish moss, buried and then dug up before rot set in, was dried and used for mattresses. Featherbeds were luxuries to be anticipated for the future. If the trunk that Emily had brought from Kentucky contained no cooking equipment, plain supplies of this kind could be bought in Bevilport or made from wood on the place. The dishes from the trunk, while too great in sentimental value for everyday use, were things to display proudly to visitors, such as the preacher when he called, usually in the middle of the week. And the pride of the house, the silver-plated tea service which Nancy Allen had packed in the trunk, was carefully polished with ashes, lending a strange incongruity to the roughness of the things that it reflected. Emily's house was given a civilized air by the items that her mother and Frances provided her with, things which she and Andrew could not buy.

Andrew was away from home most of February, March, and April, 1846, for during that time he took three flatboats to Sabine Pass. Even when he was at home he was probably so occupied with the construction of the boats and the management of his accounts that Emily saw him only at mealtimes and at night. In the daylight hours Andrew and his men were cutting timber in the woods or working on the flatboats at the riverbank. If something urgent arose, requiring more than a woman's strength, Emily could call one of the men for help; but as a rule, business was business and it was not to be mingled with domestic activities.

Being alone was no novelty to Texas wives, for it was an experience that even the most pampered women grew accustomed to. At breakfast, lunch, and supper Ann hauled buckets of food to the woods where the men were working. Her approach was the signal for Andrew to join his wife and take his meal with her in the quiet of the cabin. For two people so involved in their individual responsibilities, moments together were important. It was to extend and enrich those moments that they labored.

Toward the end of April, Andrew decided to build the *Jasper*. That

he selected this particular month might have been more than coincidence, in that the baby was due before long. The routine of the house
continued as it had been, with Ann attending to the heavy work, such
as washing, while Emily directed. Andrew kept a rigid schedule with
his employees on the riverbank and the *Jasper* took shape.

Finishing touches were being put on the keelboat late in May when
Frances and Mammy Silla trotted their mules up the sandy road to
take possession of the cabin. May 30, the cabin doors and shutters were
opened and Andrew was permitted inside to see his daughter, who was
born that morning. From her bed Emily named the child Nancy, for
Nancy Allen.

A week later Andrew headed the *Jasper* and a flatboat toward the
coast. Solid profits had been made from the spring trips and it was time
to turn part of those profits into necessities for the cabin. Emily spoke
while Andrew wrote in his account book: [22]

> 2 musketoe Bars, 2 bed blankets
> 1 bolt quilt lining, 1 bolt domestic
> 8 yds. red flannel, 6 yds. bleached domestic
> 6 yds apron check, 6 gingham handkerchiefs.
> 6 yds calico, 8 yds, calico fine for Ft.
> 1 doz. shirt buttons, 6 doz, pants buttons.
> 1 doz. spools thread assorted red, green, and white.
> 1 summer coat. shoes for Emily
> 1' doz. plates. 1 doz. cups & saucers, 1 set knives and forks,
> ½ doz. tea spoons, ½ doz. table spoons.
> ½ doz. dishes assorted, 2 pitchers, 1½ doz. glasses.
> 1 oven & lid, 1 skillet & lid, 1 dinner pot, 1 coffee pot,
> 1 coffee mill, 100 lbs. coffee.

The list was a good account of the needs of a backwoods wife who, in
an effort to make her home comfortable, had exhausted the uses of
available things and had to supplement her creativity with store-bought
items. Many an unbearable night could be made more restful by hanging a mosquito bar—a thin cloth net—around the bed, and likewise,
a covered oven could better the quality of cornbread. Necessities dominated Emily's list, but nicer, less needed things such as tableware and
good calico evidenced that the Smyth's fortunes had improved in these
past five months on Indian Creek.

A man in a boat passing this spot could look with interest at the cabin

[22] Account book, 1846. AFS MSS.

on the bank in its clearing. Chickens, ducks, the cow, and the work animals, the vegetable garden, and perhaps a few flowers blooming beside the door all hinted of good times. Rowing on, watching the scene disappear around a wooded bend, many a Texan could be envious.

V

Andrew's and Emily's letters to their parents and friends were filled with enthusiastic reports of the state of Texas. Captain Smyth, still at his mill on Big Nance Creek, was again interested in moving west.[23] He had remarried since Andrew left home eleven years before, and was rearing more sons and daughters. Andrew's younger brother, Constantine—called Conse—was already preparing to visit Texas in hopes of finding business opportunities. In 1844 Sarah, Andrew's sister, had married a Moulton man named Green Wallace, who had taken her to Cherokee County, not far northwest of Jasper County. George's success had somewhat dazzled his Alabama relatives, for it seemed really magnificent when described in letters.

With two sons enjoying good times in Texas, Captain Smyth found remaining on Big Nance Creek more difficult than ever. Benjamin and Nancy Allen were no less consumed with Texas fever. In winter letters to Andrew and Emily they told of plans of being in Texas by spring, and when spring came they moved the time of departure to summer. Neither the Smyths nor the Allens seemed to realize that there were bad aspects to offset, if not overpower, the good promises of the Lone Star.

Some new Texans were having terrible experiences in the wilderness. Sarah Smyth Wallace wrote to Andrew and Emily from Cherokee County:[24]

My health is very bad but my troubles are worse. Separation from friends by death and distance proves almost too much for me I have lost my dear little Malcomb he died the 27 July after a painful illness of six days his dear little body lies food for worms in the wild woods of Texas without some alteration I shall soon follow him.

Sarah's husband, Green, had this to add more than a year later:[25]

[23] M. Constantine Smyth, Moulton, Alabama, to Andrew F. Smyth, March 1, 1847. AFS MSS.

[24] Sarah Wallace, Cherokee County, Texas, to Emily Allen Smyth, July 14, 1846. AFS MSS.

[25] Green Wallace, Cherokee County, Texas, to Andrew and Emily Smyth, January 24, 1846. AFS MSS.

. . . If I cannot better myself I shall leave Texas. We labor under too many disadvantages here it is about 140 miles to Shreveport which is the nearest place of navagation. Against I get my cotton there and then back I can put what remaining in a coffee sack and if I can do no better I cannot do much worse.

The Wallaces were by no means the only Texans experiencing hard times. Perhaps Andrew and Emily wrote their parents describing the poor health, poverty, and general hardships which sometimes followed people from the moment they stepped across the Sabine until the day several years later when they moved on, blind and believing, to another promised land. At any rate, the Smyths and the Allens looked around themselves and must have felt more contented than before, for they abandoned their notions of living in Texas.[26]

In the year 1846 Jasper County was reduced to about half its original size when Newton County was established between the town of Jasper and the Sabine River. As it had been, Jasper County was large, and although the county seat was centrally located, bad roads made it hard for the scattered population to attend court days and other important events. Western Jasper County's interests centered in the Angelina and Neches Rivers, while the eastern part of the county relied upon the Sabine, so that a separation seemed logical. With the exception of merchants and men in Andrew's line of business, the 797 white residents of Jasper County were farmers or were connected in some way with agriculture, primarily the planting of cotton. The 251 Negroes in the county were all slaves, who worked for masters in various capacities.[27] For January, 1847, the overall picture was one of prosperity, which people like Green Wallace, knowing poor times elsewhere, noticed with some envy.[28]

Andrew Smyth was doing well in the flatboat and keelboat business. His account books thickened with each trip; his house beside the river and the creek was simple, but it was a place to be proud of, even if it was not entirely his. Emily had adjusted to this rough way of life and had softened it somewhat with her domestic ingenuity.

In late July or early August little Nancy would have a brother or sister. Emily, thinking of the future, had already said that a new house

26 M. Constantine Smyth, Moulton, Alabama, to Andrew F. Smyth, October 26, 1847; Nancy and Benjamin Allen, Daviess County, Kentucky, to Andrew and Emily Smyth, May 1, 1847. AFS MSS.

27 H. Bailey Carroll, "Texas Collection," *Southwestern Historical Quarterly*, L (1946), 117.

28 Green Wallace, Cherokee, County, Texas, to Andrew F. Smyth, January 19, 1847. AFS MSS.

should be built farther back from the river to accommodate the growing household. And Emily had conquered every fear but that of the whirlpool, which still horrified her. She wanted the new house to be out of the way of the water; she wanted the whirlpool to be far away from the children, who in a few years would be playing in the yard.

Realizing that a freight business could prosper only when crops were good, Andrew wished to extend his interests into other, more substantial fields. Certain insects were already making themselves known in the cotton fields and bad crops had occurred here and there. The time had been when a few crop failures were no worry to a riverman. Then, though, the problem had not been as threatening as it was now, with the insects. Andrew's family, he determined, must not want for comforts simply because of a universal crop failure.

He had always had a distrust of cotton, calling it fickle. His lack of confidence was one reason why he had preferred not to be a planter in the first place. Now he wanted to take every precaution against being hurt by the cotton crisis which seemed to be on its way. On his trips to Sabine Pass he had never had difficulty in selling flatboats for lumber. Residents of the marshy Gulf coast area needed the wood for their houses and stores, and they had no way of getting such materials close at hand. For some time Andrew had planned to start shipping loads of lumber downriver. He said that then he would be safe, no matter what the cotton crops did.

Directly related to his plans for selling cut timber in Sabine Pass was his growing awareness of the need for milled lumber there in Jasper County. Wood was abundant, but too few places were available where one could have it finished as suitable building material for an up-to-date structure. Evidently the few sawmills in the county had no easy time supplying the demand. William A. Ferguson in a note to Andrew advised, ". . . nowhere can a lumber mill be operated [to] greater advantage than at Jasper County."[29] Ferguson lived in Tyler County, which was a part of old Liberty County, just across the Neches from George's Walnut Run farm and embracing Andrew's Republic of Texas land claim near Town Bluff.

A gregarious, likable man who loved card games and church meetings with equal devotion, William A. Ferguson was constantly involved in business ventures with various merchants at the Pass and landowners

[29] William A. Ferguson, Jasper, Texas, to Andrew F. Smyth, June 26, 1847. AFS MSS.

in the upcountry. Business was an enjoyable gamble with Ferguson, a man whose name appeared on the salary list now and then in Andrew's account book because some investment had left him temporarily without money.

Andrew and Ferguson were the best of friends and apparently Andrew attributed great worth to his friend's opinion. Their friendship bred a trust that Andrew would regret. During the winter and spring Andrew filled the margins of his notebooks with scribblings concerning sawmills.

Patrick Hussey was not pressing for his money for the land, but Andrew realized that the price would rise with each improvement that he made on the site. Gradually he had reached a position where the note could be paid in part, and it was, regularly. But the bulk remained unpaid.

Andrew decided to expand his business enterprises, while still making the trips to the coast with the *Jasper* and flatboats. He had no reason to discontinue the old business, because it was profitable and Andrew liked the river life; he now planned how he would divide his time and increase his number of employees. The additional cash, he figured, would more than compensate for the additional effort. Sometime shortly before the summer of 1847 the sawmill on Indian Creek was built.

7. Andrew Farney Smyth at thirty was a miller, an occupation that harkened memories of the childhood which a struggling Alabama mill had hurried to an end, sending an ambitious boy to Texas. This sawmill in Jasper County, he hoped, would have a more profitable history than the gristmill of his youth.

I

The sawmill was situated a short distance up from the mouth of Indian Creek, in sight of the cabin. At the spot where Andrew built the mill, the creek rushed faster than usual, heading down an incline toward the Angelina. The origin of the saw's power was in this swift current.

Structurally the mill had a wooden frame and a shake roof, with a floor extending over the current of the creek. The focal point of the whole building was the wafer-like steel saw. In the current was a waterwheel, which transmitted power from the creek to the saw through a series of invigorating axles and wheels; given life in this manner, the saw could cut logs quickly and effectively into lumber.

William A. Ferguson had strong business ties with a Sabine Pass merchant named Alexander, who, like most coastal merchants, always needed backwoods products. Ferguson and Alexander loaned Andrew small amounts of money for equipment during the building of the mill and they were repaid in finished lumber, which undoubtedly found its way to Sabine Pass. Perhaps the loans had come from Alexander through Ferguson to Andrew in the first place. It is certain that when the demand for a certain product was great, merchants were eager to supply it, even when the risks involved were many. Lumber was one of the most pressing needs of the coastal prairies.

Andrew's trips downriver with the keelboat and flatboats did not stop while the mill was being built. He made from $175 to $250 from each trip, depending upon the amount of cotton shipped and the number of orders which he could fill for merchandise.[1] This fairly dependable income was vital, for five men were hired to work on the boats and four were employed at the mill, besides the occasional Negro who was paid

[1] Andrew F. Smyth account book and business papers, 1847. AFS MSS.

to help Emily at home. None of the workers were luxuries. They were all needed for one specific purpose or another. In addition, the purchase of tools had been a substantial investment in the beginning, and with each trip downriver new ones needed to be bought to supply the growing labor force or to replace items broken during construction.

Pole houses and, later, log houses had been built for the employees some distance downriver near the place where the boats were built, costing Andrew man hours, for which he was paying dearly. The workmen did not cook for themselves since Emily found that she could save money by preparing food at the cabin and sending it over to their quarters.

Such expenses as these left Andrew with a smaller profit than the farmers probably imagined that he made.

When Andrew was downriver, an overseer—usually Ferguson when he was in the county—supervised work at the mill. In April, Andrew and Ferguson speculated in buying Jasper County cotton and selling it in New Orleans. Though apparently the return from this venture hardly covered Andrew's expenses in both time and money, the mill was kept in operation by a new employee named Jerry Delaney, a tall, austere man from Town Bluff. Jerry proved to be an asset to Andrew; he preferred working for a salary rather than a percentage of the intake, and through his serious dedication to everything he did, he grew in Andrew's estimation. It was good, too, for Emily to have a dependable person so near when Andrew was gone. They both liked Jerry Delaney, with good reason. He was well worth fifteen dollars a month and room and board.[2]

More and more the place beside the creek and the river became a center of activity, the scene of busy progress. Business costs, together with the small expenses of the household, claimed most of the income, which, until the mill went into operation, was entirely from the river enterprises. Still, Andrew and Emily were already enjoying some of the comforts which they had hoped for. If times stayed good, more would come.

On the 1,060 acres Andrew found a supply of any kind of timber that he wanted. In May, 1847, his account books began to fill with orders for lumber, mostly cypress and pine, the desirable building materials. A flood of requests came for clapboards. Besides being more nearly windproof, a clapboard house was a sign of prosperity, and people who could afford it were ready to modernize their homes with this better siding. Rather than building new houses, it was common to cover the

2 *Ibid.*

older log structures with clapboards, thus giving the wanted effect with a minimum expense. Andrew furnished lumber for buildings in Jasper and Bevilport, alike.

Jasper was a hamlet of forty inhabitants, while Bevilport, primarily a business center for farmers and merchants, had fewer permanent residents but did have streets which were deceptively crowded during most of the day.

Not far from the Smyth's cabin and mill was a long, wide swamp thick with cypress trees. For a month or so each year the swamp was dry enough to walk in. During the dry time Andrew and his hired men cut a passage through the cypress forest, allowing the felled trees to remain on the ground. When the water rose again these trees, stripped of their branches, were floated to a place nearest the mill and pulled to dry ground, where they were stacked to await the milling process. Forest pines yielded more readily to the axe than did the cypress of the swamp and they were less awkward to handle. In dense woods such as those on Andrew's land the pines were tall, bare except at the top of limbs, where was the foliage, which was chopped away so that the logs could be dragged by oxen to the mill with little trouble. An irregular sand road extended between Bevilport and Andrew's improvements on the riverbank. Passing through the center of the property, this road simplified log hauling to some degree, as well as being a worn passage into which logging roads could lead.

At the mill different sizes of clapboards, flooring, joists, and studs were cut to order from the heart of the tree. Timber was in such abundance that anything but the best was used for firewood or was discarded. Wide boards for heavy construction were sawed in slabs from the logs, while, for use in making the tapered clapboards, logs were sliced deep from end to end all the way around, a process which from the butt of the log resembled the slicing of a pie.[3] The fresh-milled lumber was then planed by hand and stacked upright, tepee style, to be seasoned over a smoldering fire. Depending upon the weather, the lumber was usually ready for sale in about three weeks. Andrew charged three dollars per hundred feet for pine and oak and from five to eight dollars for good cypress.[4]

Pine, oak, and cypress were the main woods handled at the sawmill, but now and then Andrew noted an order for cherry, walnut, or black

[3] Eric Sloane, *American Yesterday,* p. 42.
[4] Account book and sawmill papers, 1847–1849. AFS MSS.

gum to be used in furniture making. So frequent were the demands of local customers that very little of his lumber seems to have gone into the Sabine Pass trade, though Andrew had definite plans to send shipments there as soon as he could.

In building the mill, he had made a wise move. His decision to construct it had been quick, unlike him. But these years of experience in business had matured his judgment so that he felt able to recognize a good thing when he saw it. This time he had indeed been correct.

II

The most exciting event since annexation was the Mexican War. Texans, not far removed from the Revolution, had shown a great interest in this war, contributing some 8,000 soldiers.

When the reorganized Jasper Volunteers set out for the Rio Grande, Andrew was not with them. To fight the Mexicans again was truly a fashionable thing, but Andrew was too busy at home.[5] He did not like wars or the wastes that they left behind, and, as it happened, his mill, his boats, and his family needed him, he felt, more than did the Jasper Volunteers. Since Andrew did not even subscribe to a newspaper, any information that he had about General Zachary Taylor's regular army and the thousands of volunteers came from letters and by word of mouth.[6]

During these active days of the late 1840's the Smyths enjoyed several guests from out of state. Andrew's brother, Conse, at twenty-two, came to Texas in July, 1847, to look into the possibilities of establishing himself in a business. A favorite of George and Andrew's, Conse was a dark, handsome youth who was more interested in the benefits of money than in the methods of making it. His quick wit and flourish of manner gave him a certain adeptness, mainly for borrowing money with which to impress his newest friends in the short interim before they became his creditors.

The amiable Conse, always ready to give his practical brothers the most elegant advice, bid the Smyths goodbye at the end of July after a well-rounded tour of the state. If another volunteer company left the Moulton vicinity to fight in the Mexican War, he surely wanted to be there to join up. It was really a shame that this Texas visit came at the

5 Temple Darnell, Galveston, Texas, to Andrew F. Smyth, June, 1847.
6 Ibid.

time the main company left. He agreed before he went home that he would soon pay his Texas debts, with large bonuses.[7] By the last part of the agreement, Andrew and George sensed that they had best settle these matters of money themselves.

Not long after Conse left, Emily gave birth to a second daughter. It was decided that the child be named Susannah, after Andrew's mother, and called Susan. Nancy Allen had stayed away when her namesake was born, but now, twice a grandmother, the temptation was too great.

She wrote asking when would be a good time to come to Texas. Emily received the letter at about the time she was able to resume the routine of her household. Hurriedly, she wrote an answer, telling her mother that she, the children, and Ann would go to Kentucky for a while, then accompany Nancy to Texas, where she could stay as long as she pleased. William Allen, the teen-aged son of Emily's cousin by that same name was being sent from Jasper County by his father for a visit with relatives in Kentucky. Andrew seems to have made no objections to his wife's plans, though he suggested that William travel with her. During October he drove the five of them in a wagon to Logansport, Louisiana, and booked passage for Kentucky by way of the Red River, New Orleans, and the Mississippi to the Ohio.[8] The steamer slid out of sight.

Andrew returned home to his business affairs. Emily extended her vacation into two, then three, months; Andrew was considerably annoyed. He depended upon her probably more than he had realized. At several desperate times in Emily's absence he rode to the Walnut Run farm and brought Mammy Silla back to the cabin to tidy things up. When Christmas came and Emily showed no signs of coming home, he hired a cook.[9] Sometime later, beside the date of Easter Sunday in his account book, he scrawled "lonely here."

The Mexican War ended February 2, 1848, with a treaty by which Mexico surrendered all claims to Texas and recognized the Rio Grande as the boundary between herself and Texas. Back home, the Jasper Volunteers would tell gaudy war tales which, in time, even they might believe. The stories had to be at least as good as those told by the veterans of 1836, who still thought that their exploits were the greatest examples of heroism in modern times. But one consolation was that the conversation on the store porches and the courthouse square would be given

[7] M. Constantine Smyth, Moulton, Alabama, to Andrew F. Smyth, June 21, 1847. AFS MSS.

[8] Account book, 1847; personal accounts, 1847–1848. AFS MSS.

[9] Ibid.

new spirit. The story tellers of the Revolution had reigned there for twelve years. It was time for a change.

Andrew Smyth's home was isolated from other people. Bevilport was not far away and, in fact, Andrew's south land line touched the Bevilport townsite, though all but the riverfront of that townsite was woods. A man who came to see Andrew on business might occasionally bring his wife along so that she could call on Emily, if Emily was at home. More often than not, the Smyths were removed from social activity, even of this limited kind. Guests ordinarily stayed overnight or longer when they came, because the hosts, after having only their workers for company, were eager to talk to someone with whom they felt on equal footing.

To attend a ball, say, at George's, two full days were required to make the trip, visit, and then return. Most of the time, weddings, funerals, and other events involved the same amount of time. To miss two days was no small thing for a riverman and miller, and Andrew never failed to record time lost for "frivoloty" in his account book. Emily enjoyed balls and barbecues from time to time but Andrew's business so consumed him that he resented even the loss of Sundays.

From the excitement of his boats or mill, Andrew could go home to the comfort of a good meal and be amused by his children and the conversation of his wife. That was to Andrew a stimulating life. Financial achievement was very important to him; little recreation was needed. For Emily, duties at the cabin in a while lost their newness and she anticipated the entertainments in the county.[10] Andrew simply did not want to give time to such things. And perhaps his lack of consideration was one reason why Emily's visit to Kentucky continued as the months of 1848 wore on. Andrew, she knew, sometimes could not be told things in words. So irritated did he become if business projects were not handled properly by his employees, that he flew into rages, demanding that the work be done over to his satisfaction. Uproars he enjoyed, because he had never been able to afford them before. Emily knew her husband's temper and could avoid the rare but furious outbursts by handling him in her own way.

Early in April, Emily wrote that she was coming home in the following month, the seventh of her absence. Andrew brought the *Jasper* upriver with a full cargo of merchandise in mid-May and listed among

10 Andrew F. Smyth, Bevilport, Texas, to William A. Ferguson, May 5, 1847. AFS MSS.

his own purchases a bolt of blue brocade, "for my wife." He arranged for a wagon and mules in which to travel to the Red River, where he was to meet Emily and the children. May 30 he wrote George that he was "very tired of living a widower."[11]

Six people greeted Andrew from the steamer that early June morning: Emily and the girls, William Allen, Ann, and Nancy Allen, whom he had probably not expected to come, since Emily's visit in Kentucky had been so long. In the wagon a place was made for baby Susan, while everyone else crowded in as best they could. If Emily had tried to prove a point, it was proven, for it is unlikely that there was a happier man in East Texas at that moment than Andrew Smyth, who flipped the leather lines as the mules pulled the wagon to the cabin beside the creek and the river.

III

When an evangelist stopped in the county a centrally located grove was selected where the people could come and camp among the trees, spending perhaps three or four days, just to hear the "preaching."[12] Inspired by the evangelist's words, they would return home and read their Bibles with greater care.

Andrew, Emily, their daughters, Nancy Allen, and the George W. Smyth children attended such a four-day meeting in November of 1848.[13] It was a beautiful time of the year, the leaves at their peak of color, the air so crisp that Andrew probably took his flatboat tent along and set it up over a bed of pine needles to protect his family from the chill of the fall evenings. All day long, beginning after an early-morning breakfast, the evangelist preached to his audience, which grew or diminished according to his abilities. At noon the women began bringing every imaginable kind of food to the tables that the men had made from timbers; when most of the food was consumed the entire camp meeting napped until about four, and then the preaching resumed, lasting by the light of a bonfire until late in the evening.

The successful evangelist was something of a showman, of necessity. Part of his appeal was in his dramatic presentation, the way he fright-

[11] Andrew F. Smyth, Jasper County, Texas, to George W. Smyth, May 30, 1848. GWS MSS, UTA.

[12] William Tellis Parmer, *Seventy-Five Years in Nacogdoches: A History of the First Baptist Church*, p. 38.

[13] Frances Grigsby Smyth, Jasper, Texas, to George W. Smyth, November 6, 1848. GWS MSS, UTA.

ened his listeners with predictions of Hell and damnation, should they continue their evil ways. Few revivals escaped a visitation from pranksters, who delighted in sending a wild horse with his tail on fire through the crowd, or the inevitable throwing of skunks on the scene at a particularly moving moment. Some ministers were capable of answering these interruptions and remaining dignified, and those were the ones who stayed in business.

As the revivals moved into the third and fourth days, participants here and there began to react to the evangelist's plea to surrender to the Lord. Young girls were not the only people to cry, scream, and make a conspicuous display over being saved. Grown men and aged grandmothers saw the light with equal fervor. Emily recalled that once Jerry Delaney came to a camp meeting to deliver a message to Andrew and became so involved with the proceedings that he vowed before the entire assembly to attend church for the rest of his life. He changed his mind later on.

A camp meeting was more than a time of colorful testimony. It was not only an event where souls were purified, even if ostensibly that was its purpose. The meetings in the woods were times when people like the Smyths could remove themselves for a moment from the responsibilities and hardships of routine, and at the same time release tensions and see that there was a purpose to life, above merely existing. They were in this new country to find the good life of earthly achievement. In religion they saw another kind of good life, one which made the everyday struggle toward the jackpot seem less significant.

The Lord was good to those who loved Him, true enough, but the real reward of the Godly way was at the end of life. Happenings of the days should not turn men from the face of God, because as men they were not capable of judging God's acts; when life was over, understanding in a kingdom where all was good would be offered—a wonderful philosophy, if it could be believed. For many, this belief was the only possible relief from the frustrations of the promised land of Texas.

Frontier Christianity fortified those who were weary. The preacher could tell Sarah Wallace that her baby Malcomb's death was simply "God's will," which, since it could not be questioned, was somehow satisfactory. The pioneers were people who believed readily, believed that raw woods could be made into earthly fortunes, believed that they could endure hardships even beyond the instant when they fell under the pressure; and they died still believing. They had faith in God when the matter was presented to them. Providence loomed as a mountain too high to climb, too distant to really see, yet a mountain ready to protect those who labored in the right way at its feet. The right way was in the Bible. Those loyal workers could anticipate Eden when their lives were ended. In Eden, the preachers swore, would be the good life in all its delicious—if undefined—splendors. The world often went back on its promises; God did not.

Only two churches were represented in Jasper County—the Baptist and the Methodist. Both Andrew and Emily had been reared as Presbyterians; but because there was no Presbyterian church in the vicinity they became Baptists, and devout ones, as most of the people in their area were.

Circuit riders, traveling through, preached where a church house had been erected or in some other place if the congregation did not have a building. When services were held they lasted all day, with a lunch served "on the ground," somewhat in the manner of a camp meeting.

By summer, 1848, a congregation had gathered in the Indian Creek neighborhood. Growing tired of the long ride to attend church elsewhere, the people of Indian Creek planned to build a church on high ground beside the creek and to provide space for a graveyard nearby. A site was selected adjoining Andrew's property, at the foot of a long, gradual hill. Andrew was given charge of the building—a likely position for the owner of a sawmill.

This particular Baptist church, few of its members residents of towns or settlements, had its extremists who touched puritanism and those who took their religion quietly, just as some of its people could read and write, while others could not. It was not so different from any other backwoods church, and its preacher, feeling free to discuss anything that he pleased from the pulpit, was convinced that all was in the realm of religion.

Emily attended church each time that a service was held and that was anytime a preacher could be found. Dedicated to her own responsibilities in life, she lacked the worries which the hard country life gave some women. The church was a duty to her, a worthwhile part of one's existence, and, seeing that she had much to be thankful for, she believed sincerely, if blindly. On meeting days she dressed her children and with a basket of food drove the old buggy that Andrew had bought her to the place where the service was to be held. When Andrew was at home he went, too, and even Ann was required to go and sit in the place reserved for slaves.

Like Emily, Andrew felt a dutiful attachment to the church. But any closeness that he felt was due to respect for his mother's beliefs and, later, Emily's. God to him was not dynamically present, directing every moment of every hour. The experiences of his work gave him an impression of life somewhat different from that of his wife.

Once, on a river trip, his party of eight had been asleep in a tent on the flatboat when a tree fell from the bank and crushed one of his workers and a woman who was along as a passenger. The tragedy occurred at a secluded part of the river. The next morning the man and the woman were buried in the woods and the event was related to the sheriff at the next town, many miles downriver.[14] The investigation that was carried on was mere formality. The two had died uselessly, unaware of why, there in a strange place, a lonely forest far from anything they knew or had known.

Such happenings seemed unnecessarily cruel to Andrew. He saw too much of this kind of waste to be able to think that there could be purpose behind any of it. A practical man could see very little Godliness in the low life of the Galveston waterfront, or reason why a so-called kind God would permit criminals to wander among honest folk. Then, in contrast to these experiences he went to his home and saw goodness and a clean life, which were always waiting for him at the end of a harrowing journey. The resultant philosophy was not unique.

Andrew felt that some men selected a good life and some did not. Some of the rowdiest rivermen were good people in their relations with others, while he knew respected planters who were scoundrels. God had very little to do with it, directly. A wise man kept his sins moderate and followed the general guidelines of the Bible and his own common sense, which after all were the best ways, and he could count on going to paradise, if there was one. God really couldn't ask more and might expect less, considering the world which he put men in.

George W. Smyth, with Frances and their seven children, still enjoyed comforts, if not luxuries, at the farm on Walnut Run. His interest in government was very much alive and his position in the county was that of an accomplished politician.

The provisions of annexation had stipulated that Texans could deal with their public lands as they saw fit, a matter involving millions of acres, some of which had already been disposed of. George kept a lively correspondence with various people, exchanging ideas and opinions, and he had much to say about these public lands. His experience in land

[14] Andrew F. Smyth, Galveston, Texas, to George W. Smyth, 1848. GWS MSS, UTA.

transactions and surveying, together with his reputation among politicians, had prompted the state legislature to appoint him commissioner of the General Land Office in March, 1848, to finish the term of Robert Witherspoon, who had died.

Under regular circumstances this office was filled by a general election. As land commissioner, George was to look after the state's interests in the disposition of the many public sections of land and to see that the state received the best possible price when the land was sold. In the summer of 1848, therefore, he was in Austin, assuming the duties of the office.

In his brother's absence Andrew kept a watchful eye on the management of the Walnut Run farm. The *Jasper* and the flatboats stopped at the Walnut Run farm landing to take any orders for merchandise that Frances might want filled. Frances was adept in matters of business and carried on a number of building projects at home, probably in accordance with her husband's plans. All her lumber was from the mill on Indian Creek. Once each month, after Andrew had spent several days examining the Walnut Run operations, he wrote George a long letter describing in detail what he had observed and what changes, if any, he had made. He felt a deep dedication to any service that he might perform for his brother. It would be a long time before George was home again to stay, for he had to stand an election in August of the next year for the office he now held.

Nancy Allen's visit with her daughter came to a close in November. She had been away from home many months. Emily was to have another child, and while Nancy wanted to stay until early summer when the child was expected, she realized that it was time to leave now. Andrew had been very kind in seeing that she accompanied Emily and him to social events in the county, though he had been gone from home from time to time on trips downriver. Her gentle way of accepting things as they were had endeared her to Andrew, who had probably been reluctant to bring his mother-in-law to this clearing in the woods. In the buggy he drove her northeast of Jasper to a landing on the Red River, where she waited several days for the next New Orleans bound steamer.

On New Year's Day, safely at home, she wrote of her journey: [15]

Mr. Smyth you know you left me at Grantico on Friday evening I cannot describe my feelings on parting with you they were bad enough I assure you notwithstanding I was the only white female there was about the house no person

[15] Nancy Allen, Daviess County, Kentucky, to Andrew and Emily Smyth, January 1, 1849. AFS MSS.

could be treated with more politeness and respect than I was   our fare was excellent my bill was one dollar and a half   We left there on Sunday morning 2 oclock on board the Satoma an excellent boat . . .   My passage was 8 dollars to New Orleans   we landed their Tuesday evening 2 oclock and left at 4 the same on board the General Scot Passage 12 dollars a very good boat   we were 8 days from New Orleans home we landed too hours before day on Wednesday morning . . .   It rained on us til day and was verry cold and as dark as it could be . . .   they sent a horse for me and cart for my baggage . . .   Black and white ran to meet me.

Nancy had thoroughly enjoyed her visit to Texas, but she left firmly convinced that the Allens were better off living in Kentucky.[16]

IV

Andrew worked through the winter and spring of 1849, attending to what he had and considering new projects to undertake. With the management of the mill to handle, he did not travel to Sabine Pass as frequently as he had in the past few years. He knew what that first steamboat whistle at Bevilport last January had meant and would mean to the career of the *Jasper*.[17] At least twice in the spring he had built flatboats for William A. Ferguson, who took the boats downriver, paying Andrew on a percentage basis.[18] No overwhelming profits were being realized from these enterprises, but as the mill became more firmly established, business improved. In fact, so much improvement had been noticed that some agreement should soon be reached with Patrick Hussey about purchasing the land. Patrick had not yet decided upon a final price though Andrew had been paying him small amounts over the years.

Emily stayed at home during her third pregnancy, directing Ann in the care of beehives, chickens, and the other things about the clearing. Within the cabin were a loom and a spinning wheel. Emily did the weaving herself. When Andrew had a large order to fill at the mill he often worked after dark by torchlight. Emily, on those nights, left Ann with the children and had her loom carried to the mill, where she would remain, weaving, while her husband planed lumber or operated the saw. The leaping fire from a pine knot cast a yellow glow on their work as

16 Nancy Allen, Daviess County, Kentucky, to Emily Smyth, December 25, 1849. AFS MSS.

17 William Allen, Jasper County, Texas, to George W. Smyth, January 8, 1849. GWS MSS, UTA.

18 William A. Ferguson, Town Bluff, Texas, to Andrew F. Smyth, November 28, 1848; business papers of Andrew F. Smyth, 1849. AFS MSS.

they talked, scarcely looking at one another, into the late hours of the night; Ann dozed at the cabin and the employees of the mill were fast asleep in their quarters beyond the fringes of the light.

The child, a daughter, was born May 28. They named her Araminta, after no one in particular, and hoped that their next child would be a boy.

Hearing that both Nancy Allen and Captain Smyth were seriously ill, Andrew and Emily traveled from Jasper County soon after Araminta was born. They left the children with Frances. In early June they arrived at the Allens and spent two weeks there. Finding Nancy much improved in health, they went to Alabama to visit for three weeks at the gristmill on Big Nance Creek. Captain Smyth's condition did not better during that time, but they felt that they could stay no longer.

The captain, too old now to work in his mill, had turned its operations over to his younger sons, Andrew's brothers and half-brothers. Andrew could do nothing to help ease the situation, but he was glad he had come, if only to let his father have the satisfaction of knowing that he had kept the promise he had made in the autumn of 1835. The promise to return to Big Nance Creek he had not forgotten. Traveling by steamer, Andrew and Emily were at home by late August, working and taking part in the social activities of the Indian Creek neighborhood.

Sometime that summer the Indian Creek church was built. It was a slightly rectangular structure, tall, angular, built of lumber which Andrew had contributed. Windows were spaced along the sides, and double front doors and a huge fireplace faced each other from the two ends of the single room.[19] The walls were cypress clapboards, covered inside with pine. The floors were of pine and there is some indication that the interior was painted pale green; if so, it was a luxurious building, for paint was not common to the backwoods. Slanting from the building to the rust-colored waters of the creek was the cemetery, empty and covered with pine needles and scattered cedars, newly planted.

The Smyths' cabin was about a mile down the creek from the church, although their land extended to the churchyard.

This building, convenient for most of the people in the neighborhood, would serve as a church, school, and meeting house for those who lived near it. The erection of such a house was evidence that the area was settled enough to have an eye on another kind of progress beyond the

[19] Floorplans for the Indian Creek Church dated June, 1849. The plan suggests that there was a gallery, which probably accommodated slaves, providing there was such a gallery. AFS MSS.

want of land and good cotton. On a certain Sunday each month people on foot, in wagons, on horseback, or in buggies moved toward the finished church building, their lunches packed in buckets or baskets. Over the years this was repeated monthly, in all kinds of weather. The cedars grew tall and shaded the lines of brick and marble and wooden grave markers that appeared as the years went by. At Indian Creek Church could be felt the sense of belonging, which had at last come with the good and bad of the new land.

V

George was elected land commissioner by the people in the August election and when the excitement of the election was over, Andrew put local campaigning out of his mind and set out to cancel his debt to Patrick Hussey. A price had never been decided upon. Emily, probably inspired by her parents' large new house in Kentucky, was anxious to move from the cramped cabin.[20] On Walnut Run, Frances had added a wing to her house and had built a schoolhouse in the yard.[21] So much building was going on in the county that Emily was constantly reminded, and in turn reminded Andrew, that she needed a new house.

With a sawmill Andrew could easily build whatever Emily wanted, without much expense. But it was foolish to invest any more in this 1,060-acre farm until some arrangement was made for buying it. Patrick agreed to $1,200 for the land, and since he was Andrew's friend and customer he would take notes without interest for any length of time which Andrew wanted. Patrick was making an enormous profit but Andrew could not complain. Borrowing $200 from a Jasper merchant at 10 per cent, Andrew signed a one-year and a two-year note, each for $500, to Patrick Hussey.[22]

The transaction had hardly been completed when the courthouse in Jasper mysteriously caught fire and burned to the ground, destroying all the official records, including Andrew's deed to the "mill property."[23] Beginning at one in the morning, the rough wooden building burned

[20] Benjamin and Nancy Allen, Daviess County, Kentucky, to Mrs. Andrew Smyth, October 24, 1847. AFS MSS.

[21] William Allen, Jasper County, Texas, to George W. Smyth, December 15, 1849. GWS MSS, UTA.

[22] Cancelled notes from the purchase of the farm, 1849–1852, AFS MSS.

[23] Andrew F. Smyth, Jasper County, Texas, to George W. Smyth, November 10, 1849. GWS MSS, UTA.

faster than a bucket brigade could haul water from Sandy Creek. That same night a Jasper doctor was robbed of $240.

A suspect was arrested, but because nothing could be proven against him he remained in jail only a short time. The residents of the county took several years to recover from that fire; they would talk and speculate as to the culprit as late as the mid-1850's. Had they found the guilty party, he would have been lucky if he escaped hanging. To have lost the land records was a serious thing.

The morning after the fire the county clerk set up a table under the scorched trees by the ruined courthouse and ordered all landholders to town to refile their titles. On December 4, 1849, the deed was again signed, the 1,060 acres transferred officially to Andrew. This time would be for good.

With clear title to the land, Andrew could consider the expansion of his business and Emily would have her new house. There were many things to work for, they reminded themselves.

8. Soon after the deed was signed, work began on the outbuildings, which would surround the new house. A long, level place had been selected near the center of the property, beside the sandy road leading to the mill. Emily was so frightened of the creek and the river that the new location was something of a comfort. Bevilport was one mile away, the road was never muddy, and the nearest dangerous water was in the swamp, across the road and some three hundred yards from where the house would be. Had it been entirely up to Emily, the house would probably have been built on the road to Indian Creek Church. That road was a half mile farther from the river than the site selected but it was too far from the mill and Andrew's business activities.

I

While Andrew was not a farmer, the new house and its environs would give certain outward impressions of the agricultural life. In a district where the majority were farmers, was it not advisable to at least participate? Emily had been reared among farmers and Andrew was a sawyer, which was a polite way of saying miller. When Jasper County was younger the category of a man's business pursuits had been of little concern, for everyone was struggling to establish himself. Now, success had precipitated social classes and one did not remain on top without some effort on his own part. Farmers, not millers and not rivermen, were on the right rung of the ladder.

The new house would be a country seat, therefore, rather typical of its surroundings. Andrew was not in a special rush to finish it, because his business was doing well and the notes on the land had to be reduced whenever money was available. In fact, the majority of the income was absorbed by this debt.

Emily was pregnant again and her activities in time would be somewhat reduced. But at last she would be able to leave this place she termed "dangerous" and move to "dry ground."[1] A son named for his Uncle George was born in July, 1850. Andrew said in a note to Jerry Delaney, "I will not go to the landing today. My wife has given birth of a boy."

[1] Emily Smyth, Jasper County, Texas, to Nancy Allen, January 20, 1850. AFS MSS

II

In September, 1851, the foundation had been laid for the new house. Most of the outbuildings were already completed, having been built of logs and milled lumber. Finished were a huge, graceless barn, an enclosed carriage house, a smokehouse, and chicken houses; plans were being made for a house for Ann, as well as accommodations for the hired men.[2]

With a compass Andrew had set the main house so that it would face west, in the direction of the river. Stakes were driven in the ground in a rectangle fifty by forty feet. Within the rectangle the house was to be built. Cypress logs were crosscut and placed to be used as piers. Thick sills were hewn with a broadaxe from cypress logs, laid across the piers, and joined together with pegs of green wood. With the foundation thus built, perhaps Andrew left the site for a month or so to attend to work at the mill. When there was another slack in business he and the workmen went again to work on the house. Emily was impatient.

In the first months of 1852 the house was still no farther along than the foundation. Bricks for the chimneys had been ordered but nothing was built, probably because Andrew was busy at the mill. So active was the mill that the keelboat had not been used for many months and only flatboats loaded with cotton and manned by Holland and three Negroes were sent downriver.

As Emily's fifth child was expected sometime toward the end of the summer, she was undoubtedly more eager than ever to have her new house. On a particular busy day, little George, who was not being watched closely, crawled to the creekbank, fell into the current, and was swept into the whirlpool, where the creek joined the river. Seeing this by sheer accident, Emily plunged into the water and pulled the child to safety.

Andrew and the workers at the mill, hearing noise at the cabin, rushed to the scene. Emily announced that she would not spend another night beside the river; Andrew reminded her that the new house was not finished and that it was foolish to make such a declaration to move because of an accident which might have happened at any time during the years they had lived on the water. But Emily was not to be argued down. She put everyone to work. During the rest of the day the contents of the cabin were piled in wagons and headed up the sandy road. By late afternoon the cabin beside the creek and the river stood empty in its

[2] Andrew F. Smyth account book, 1851. AFS MSS.

clearing. Crowded and uncomfortable, the Smyths slept that night in the smokehouse, not fifty feet from the foundations of what would be their home.[3]

No time was spared in building the main house. From the foundation the frame extended upward. Pegged together, the frame served as backing for the clapboard walls and support for the shake roof. Nails were expensive and were used sparingly.

At about this time the *Jasper* disappeared from the account books. Perhaps it was dismantled and used in the house, which would explain the peculiar pieces of lumber incorporated in the building—a bowed joist here, a timber which had mortices unfilled there.

To make a door, three wide boards were pressed side by side, held together by means of wedges and pegs. The two brick fireplaces had wide, arched openings and shallow hearths. The interior finishing was still to be done when Andrew and Emily moved in, but that, they agreed, would have to be accomplished at some later date. The immediate problem was to get out of the cramped smokehouse.

From any perspective, the house was of pleasing lines, one room deep, two rooms wide, with an open hall in the center. On the west and east sides were long porches five or six steps from the ground, enclosed by banisters. Three doors opened from each room onto the porches, making the house cool in the summer, and the many glass windows, which Andrew had brought from Galveston, checked winter drafts and yet lighted the interior.

Southerners had come to call this style house the "Dog Trot House" because of the open hallway, which was a favorite loafing place for dogs. Emily, not fond of the title, insisted that her hall be called the "entry."

When there was time the yard was enclosed with a picket fence; Andrew, in a poetic gesture, chopped two gateposts from cypress logs, fashioning the tops into crude pineapples. From a book or from George or from someplace else concerned with artistic things he had found that pineapples symbolized hospitality. Emily was charmed.

The Smyth's fourth daughter was born in August, 1852, probably in the new house. She was named for her Aunt Frances, who brought her namesake a silver cup.

Andrew and Emily had planned to have a new home early in their marriage, always considering and hoping that the place beside the creek and the river was a temporary location. Within the new fenced yard

[3] Told by Emily Allen to her granddaughter, Mrs. Mary S. Horn, who related it to the author in a conversation August 22, 1962.

Emily planted flowers, shrubs, and blooming trees. A few flower beds were arranged in pleasing patterns, but the ground around them was packed hard and swept clean as often as seemed necessary. The shrubs were set in lines like cotton in the field. Cherry trees were planted down the front walk, crape myrtles followed the fence, and a variety of roses and annuals found places in the beds. Emily had no difficulty finding plants for her yard, for country women traded cuttings and bulbs all the year. Near the front porch a greenhouse was sunk, its glass roof set at the level of the ground. Brick steps led into the deep room, which had shelves for potplants and anything else that needed to be kept cool.

Gradually Ann's house was completed and the quarters for the hired men were built soon after. By Christmas, only an old Negro, a guard, lived at the river site to protect the mill and the construction area for the flatboats. The main house was yet unfinished inside, but for the time that could wait.

The new house was more nearly in keeping with the Smyths' position in the county than the cabin had been. Andrew on several occasions had served in public offices: as one of four county commissioners several years before, he had had a part in planning roads and public buildings; as district surveyor from 1850 until 1852 he had held a prominent position in Jasper County land transactions; serving as deputy surveyor between the other two offices, he had been instrumental in winning the county's claims to part of the Texas public lands for the school system.[4] These public lands were to be sold, their revenue used to support schools in the county. In addition to holding a few public offices, Andrew was continually being appointed executor of estates or guardian of this or that minor. Like his neighbors, he "and hands" had to give time to roadwork in the course of each year, for it was in this way that the county's roads were built and maintained.[5]

Business had never been better and flatboats were being sent downriver with greater regularity. Andrew did not travel with the boats most of the time, which fact he regretted. But it was always good to have new things in mind; after all, the cotton worm had done damage already and might do more.[6] Seeming never to be satisfied, even when every-

---

[4] Notice of Andrew F. Smyth's election as county commissioner in 1846; "Certificate of Election as District Surveyor," August 5, 1850; Andrew F. Smyth, Jasper County, Texas, to Judge R. C. Doom, July 7, 1851; document showing appointment as deputy surveyor, 1852. AFS MSS.

[5] Commissioners' Court Records, Jasper County, Texas, Vol. A, p. 14.

[6] Memorandum Book, 1953, Sam W. Mellon MS.

thing was going well, Andrew was thinking of opening a store in Bevil-port.

The new house saw social events which would not have been possible in the tiny cabin. When parties were held, the porches and the entry were well-covered, cool, roomy places, where country dances and an abundance of good food completed the entertainment. Although the furniture was plain and homemade, Emily mixed what she had with a few handsome things.

Late in 1852, Andrew paid the notes held by Patrick Hussey and the Jasper merchant.[7]

More and more the orders to be filled downriver included merchandise for the Smyths' own household. Bolts of bleached domestic, so many yards of calico, a sidesaddle, "four upholstered chairs," and the like appeared often in the account book. It was probably in the winter of 1853 that Andrew bought the slave, Jim, who would have duties at the house.

Following George's political convictions, Andrew had become a Democrat.[8] So well known had George become in the party that there was talk of running him for governor. He told inquiring politicians that he was not interested and gave no reason.[9] At the 1852 Democratic Convention in Tyler, Texas, slightly northwest of Jasper, George was a dark-horse candidate, nominated and elected to the United States Congress to represent the congressional district embracing Jasper County; by March, 1853, he was in Washington, sending lace and plate home to his wife, who had begged him not to accept the nomination in the first place. He had left the Land Office in 1851, his health broken, needing a long period of rest. But his political friends in 1852 were more persuasive than Frances.

Andrew and George, as always, exchanged letters regularly, speaking in slight detail of various accomplishments. They appreciated these good times.

III

The county in which Andrew and Emily lived had grown. Jasper was now a town of several hundred with stores, homes, a school, and Meth-

[7] Receipts dated November and December, 1852; Andrew's signature is torn from each receipt, as was the custom. AFS MSS.

[8] M. Constantine Smyth, Moulton, Alabama, to Andrew F. Smyth, December 13, 1846. AFS MSS.

[9] Henderson Yoakum MS.

odist and Baptist churches.[10] As in most Texas towns, the courthouse square dominated the scene. Sandy Creek meandered through the town, crossed at intervals by streets, and shaded by pines, magnolias, and other trees. Unimpressive buildings flanked the streets. The Methodist Church was a wide structure, which had a door for women and one for men, as well as an interior gallery for slaves. One of the finest buildings was the hotel, large, two-storied, with verandas; the exterior was covered with white paint, a novelty for this backwoods county seat. There were few two-story buildings, but some stores gave the effect of height with tall, false fronts, upon which the name of the firm was painted in flowery letters.

Private homes were invariably low, simple cottages with picket-enclosed yards, always kept clean of grass but tangled with blossoming plants. The rooms usually opened onto porches, which were latticed and vine hung to achieve summer coolness. Greek-revival architectural design had been only a subtle influence on the builders of Jasper. Tastes for the classical appeared at the very most in squat columns—usually unpainted—and in wooden mantels, colored to resemble marble. Country folk had learned that there were many things which an itinerant painter could do to glamourize a plain board wall.

Social life centered around the church, court days, and the holiday punch bowl, with an occasional dance or fair held in the warm months.[11] The news of the day could be read in detail in the *Eastern Texan,* the Jasper newspaper.[12] West of Jasper the Bevilport Road extended to the business town on the river. Along this nine-mile road were good farms, where lived prosperous citizens.

Andrew and Emily had built their new house a half mile off this road, not far from Bevilport. Bevilport was devoted to business, having very few private homes. Ending at the Angelina, the Bevilport Road resumed on the opposite bank to lead to Woodville, the seat of Tyler County. Horses, wagons, and people on foot could cross the narrow Angelina by paying to ride the Bevilport Ferry.

This town of Bevilport had originally been planned with neat rectangular lots and a park; as it had developed, however, it had but one street, sunken deep in the ground by heavy use and bordered by buildings.[13]

[10] Dermot H. Hardy and Ingham S. Roberts (eds.), *Historical Review of South-East Texas,* 425.

[11] Mrs. George C. O'Brien to author in conversation July 10, 1962.

[12] *Probate Minutes Book,* Vol. 1-A, Jasper County, Texas.

[13] George W. Smyth, Bevil's District, Texas, to George A. Nixon, ca. 1834. GWS MSS, UTA.

The hotel was the only painted structure. Tall, with two-story galleries and outside staircases, the hotel furnished meals and comfortable quarters for its patrons. The main stores had long porches, which extended to the river so that loading and unloading from boats would be easier. When the spring rise in the river came these stores were half in the water, half on dry land.[14] During the daytime Bevilport was busy and noisy, its stores full of people, its waterfront crowded with flatboats and keelboats, and, at high water, perhaps a steamer or two. In the stores men stood around drinking whiskey and talking of politics and farming. Ladies, dressed neatly in calico, measured yards of material and contemplated buying such things as "German silver spoons" or "Turkish combs."

While Bevilport and Jasper were the towns most closely associated with Andrew's and Emily's lives, there were other settlements and towns in the county. Near George's farm the town of Beech Grove had grown up. Zavalla, Peach Tree and Magnolia Springs, formely Pinetuckey, were other settlements. At the town of Ford's Bluff, once a regular stop for the keelboat *Jasper,* a steam sawmill had been proposed. The coming of steam-powered sawmills might account for Andrew's selling lumber only in his particular area, for the steam mills elsewhere amply supplied the parts of the Gulf coast which he had been used to dealing with.

Jasper County could offer even more of the refinements of civilization to its citizens than it had in the past. A new arrival in Jasper was George Washington Blake, master cabinetmaker, who, when there was a slack in the coffin business, created graceful pieces of furniture. Blake, a well-read, educated man, had brought his accomplished family to the town in about 1850. Among his belongings could surely be found a printed volume of furniture designs, which he copied, using the different woods available in the county. Andrew and Emily purchased some articles from him.

Having sent a wagonload of cherry and walnut to the shop in Jasper, Andrew, in due time, received from Blake a bureau, two four-poster beds, a wardrobe, and some small tables. One of the bedsteads held the pride of the house—a feather mattress. The exquisite though simple craftsmanship in these pieces greatly enhanced the interior of Andrew's residence. George Blake supplied furniture for countless people in the county, contributing elegance to that which was otherwise plain.

Among the people of the county, many names were conspicuous: Issacs, Allen, Adams, Kyle, Pace, Ryall, Lanier, Stone, Doom, all sub-

[14] Mrs. George C. O'Brien to author in a conversation July 10, 1962.

stantial planters or merchants, who were associated with Andrew just as they were with one another. Of course, Andrew had come to the county when everyone was struggling to become established; as could be expected he had known each of these families in the old days and the friendships had endured. When he had been a youth, having a prominent brother had been a great help in making friends. George found in his neighbors "all that is most valuable in the American character," and they found the same in him.[15] Andrew, entering various business ventures, from surveyor to overseer, from riverman to sawyer, had then made friends on a more solid basis. Throughout the 1850's he and Emily moved in the most enjoyable society in the county.

Going to entertainments at first only to please his wife, Andrew grew to like and even anticipate the "frivolous partys" he had once resented as interruptions. He recorded on one occasion that he had "a fine dinner" at the Fourth of July celebration, adding gleefully that "I learn this morning they danced all night."[16] Such things were foreign to his nature but he was learning to love the lighter side of life.

The flood of immigration into Texas had never really stopped. Among the new arrivals to the Bevilport neighborhood were the Seales. Joshua Seale, nearly ninety, built a plain frame house a mile from Bevilport toward Jasper; at the same time his middle-aged son, Lewis, completed a rambling two-story dwelling of logs and lumber on a high hill overlooking Bevilport and the river.[17] Between the father and son were owned thirty-two slaves, five of whom were classed as "house servants." Joshua did not farm but spent most of his time mingling in town and talking of the past, for he had turned all his business affairs over to Lewis.

Thoroughly concerned with cotton growing, Lewis was not as sociable, nor even as civil, as his father, and he occupied himself with his land and his family. At leisure moments, which were few, he liked to sit on his porch, read, and sip whiskey undisturbed. Shortly after Lewis had completed his house a delegation of ladies from the Indian Creek Church called upon him, asking for a donation to help the poor. Unfortunately, the day selected for the visit was one set aside by Lewis for quiet hours on the porch. Emily, among the callers, was shocked when he asked gruffly, "Madam, have you not learned that the best way to handle a

<hr>

[15] Richardson and Company, *The Texas Almanac for 1858*, p. 71.

[16] Andrew F. Smyth, n. p., to George W. Smyth, July 5, 1848. GWS MSS, UTA.

[17] Sketch of the Seale house made by William Seale, Sr., in 1955.

poor man is to keep him poor?" The unpleasant picture was more or less completed when the ladies found that the present Mrs. Seale had been proposed to when Lewis was riding beside her in a wagon, returning from his first wife's funeral.[18] Thus, was the first impression of Lewis Seale. Emily said in later years that she had thought him "the most uncouth man I ever hoped to meet."

One of the few men that Lewis would listen to was Uncle Dick, his slave overseer. Besides being overseer, Uncle Dick was a preacher and established a congregation of slaves one month after the Seales' arrival in Jasper County. Uncle Dick claimed that while beside his mother in a slave caravan, years before being sold to the Seales, he had seen George Washington riding down a Virginia street. And he had an amazing capacity for telling that story. True or not, Uncle Dick was no fool; he knew when to be humble, when to show spunk, when to laugh, and when to cry. In the eyes of his master and the community he could do no wrong.

Lewis and his large family joined the Indian Creek Church and in time rose somewhat in the eyes of local people. Uncle Dick had been holding services for his Negro following in a beech grove not far from the Indian Creek Church. Lewis and Joshua, having completed their residences and outbuildings, gave Uncle Dick money to build a church house of his own. In 1853 the church was finished and Uncle Dick called it Dixie Baptist Church. With a real church house now for the first time in his career as preacher, Uncle Dick embarked upon a program of conversion which amazed the community. The beech grove rocked with gospel songs all day Sundays. More from fear of the preacher than anyone else, the slaves along Indian Creek flocked into the wooden church and dared not think of missing. Their children grew up to feel the same. Of all the institutions founded in the Indian Creek community, only Dixie Church has survived.

At the first of 1854 residents of the vicinity of Indian Creek met and organized the Indian Creek Academy.[19] This was to be a college in which the various local families who contributed could enroll their children. Classes would be held in the church building and a good instructor would be hired. The plan was eventually discarded because the new Jasper Collegiate Institute had flowered with unexpected success, but for a while the organizers were enthusiastic. The Institute in

[18] Told to author by Mrs. Reese Rimer, Andrew Smyth's granddaughter, in a conversation in June, 1957.
[19] Walter Prescott Webb et al., Handbook of Texas, 877.

Jasper claimed most of the students. Finally, a grade school was placed in the church building, its management given over to Elisha, Lewis Seale's twenty-five–year–old son.[20] Schools had a hard time surviving in the county, although when one closed, parents saw that another quickly took its place. Apparently the public lands given for the support of such institutions brought only a fraction of the money needed.

Teachers were hard to find and at that were sometimes a bad investment. Frances, after a long search, engaged a teacher for the little school that she had had built at Walnut Run.

He was a Mr. Galley from outside the state, and from the start he made a poor impression upon the Smyths' friends. But since a schoolmaster was needed so desperately, everyone made special efforts to be cordial to him. The sarcastic, brooding man, who had recently reached his twenty-sixth year, was invited to an entertainment in the winter of 1850. It was an open house being held at a farm near Indian Creek Church. With perhaps too much to drink, he struck up a conversation with James Delaney, the younger brother of Jerry and a part-time employee at Andrew's mill. The teacher spoke to James purely to start an argument. In the course of the disagreement, Galley became angry, took a fire shovel from the hearth, and beat Delaney over the head violently. The crowd rushed forward; the host, after a few moments, pronounced James Delaney dead. In the confusion Mr. Galley fled to the river but was apprehended before his skiff made much progress in the current. He went away to Nacogdoches with the sheriff, leaving Frances' little school without a master.

The case of the unloved Mr. Galley was exceptionally dramatic but schoolmasters, if for more sane reasons, left about as abruptly all the time. It was a year before Frances' advertisements in the Galveston newspaper were answered by a teacher, who, by the way, later settled down and spent his life on the Walnut Run.[21]

With business going so well, Andrew and Emily had more time to be with their friends. When a new house was built, a ball usually accompanied its completion. A wedding meant a barbecue and a ball, sometimes taking two or more days to attend. Funerals were not to be missed —the friends, in fact, were duty bound to see that the corpse was properly laid out in its coffin and that animals would not harm it before burial. When a baby was born, the mother's friends always stood by.

[20] "E. D. Seale's Book, 1856." Elisha DeKalb Seale MSS.

[21] Andrew F. Smyth, Walnut Run, Jasper County, Texas, to George W. Smyth, February 16, 1850. GWS MSS, UTA.

The responsibility of home were more now. Candles and soap had to be made, vegetables had to be gathered, animals needed care, and the duties involved in hog killing always began with the first frost. Yet people like Andrew and Emily managed to participate in the social side of Texas life. Because everyone had to work, pleasure was wedged in accordingly. Andrew sometimes jotted social notes in his memorandum book: "lost 5th and 6th Dec. going to the ball at William Allens" or "spent 4th Jul at Georges."[22]

Business was of first importance, but pleasure at home was a part of everyday living. Fireside amusements varied. George W. Smyth, for instance, was fond of writing, enough so that he completed a fascinating autobiography for political friends in 1857, and wrote some poems, the best of which were humorous. When Daniel Seale, a relative of Lewis and Joshua, had a hog stolen, George preserved the incident in this manner:[23]

> Such times as these, no one can know,
> What treachery lies concealed,
> The rich, the poor, the high and low,
> All to temptations yield.
>
> Some money rules, some scruple not,
> For gain to use deceit
> Though great the crime, it seems the lot,
> Of Cameron to love meat.
>
> His hogs are few in any range,
> His mark, he has forgot,
> In Hurry, haste, 'tis true, though strange,
> Are others often shot,
>
> Attention friends while I relate,
> To you, both one and all,
> A circumstance of recent date,
> That caused poor Cameron's fall,
>
> His will, his wish, his much delight,
> To injure, wrong, and steal,
> Contrary to what's just and right,
> No longer could conceal,
>
> A short time since, 'tis true indeed,
> He killed, we must say steal,

[22] Andrew F. Smyth, "An Account Book for the Years 1848–1853." AFS MSS.
[23] George W. Smyth, one of six poems that George wrote which were discovered in the steamer trunk. AFS MSS.

Some hogs, his wife and child to feed,
Of his friend D. B. Seale,

Before he cleaned the last one killed,
Oh! bitter, baneful cup,
His heart with wonderous fear was filled,
For Daniel Seale rode up.

No time had he, to study long,
For Seale was very near,
In haste to hide a villainus wrong,
He pocketed the ear,

Though guilty he, with that concealed,
The meanest of all dogs,
He boldly said to Mr. Seale,
He had not seen his hogs,

Although said Seale, did plainly see
His hogs, all there in view,
No thought had he, that L. R. C.
An act so base would do,

How can you ever bear to face,
With acts so strange & wild,
Or press again to thine embrace,
Your tender wife and child,

Your standing lost, sunk down to woe,
From which there's no release,
'Twill haunt you, sir, where'er you go,
And mar your earthly peace,

Did earth alone this case control,
Death would a respite be,
But oh! the tortures of the soul,
Dwell in Eternity.

Although George usually wrote more serious and somewhat less effective poetry, this story of the hog thief, a familiar, much gossiped-about local happening, was circulated among his friends.

Andrew, not creative, nor concerned with being so, enjoyed maintaining a correspondence with friends outside Texas. Reading letters entertained him. Of their letters of the fifties, those from a youth named William Priest most interested Andrew and Emily. Priest had run away from home in Kentucky to visit his cousin, Emily, in Jasper County. He had spent several months with the Smyths and had expressed concern over his future, mentioning now and then that the gold rush in California appealed to him.

Andrew recalled his own worries at seventeen and there is some indication that he encouraged Priest to go to California and at least investigate the situation. Priest finally decided that he would go. And he wrote his Texas cousins from Carson's Diggings: [24]

I have maid eight hundred dollars clear and I would be glad if I could meat with an oppertunity to send it home, as it is of no use and we eather have to berry it or carry it around with us. I have mind hid in the ground about 2 feet deep   The time has been here when money was safe any where but its quite different now some think its too unsertin to. . . . dig for it and they try there hand at robbing and I think there has ben more robberies committed her in the latter summer than ever was nown the same time but Judge linch has taken the seat now and is hanging them now in all directions and this is the only law that will do any good under the present circumstances. We have Civel law but evry man has come here to make money and them that has the most money gets the best of the suit   The most of the officers are concerned with theas mine claims. . . . elections for all the state and county were held   I wish you could have seen some of the candidates   there was hundreds yes thousands of the most of them broken gamblers . . . it was laughable.

A few months before, finding no gold, he had become tired of Carson's Diggings: [25]

I am still following the same old trade digging after the growth of this country, some dias doing verry well others not much money are the ups and downs of a gold hunter washes and cooks for himself and sleaps on the ground. . . . I spent the fourth of July at work but I felt miserable all days as I knew if I was in old Jasper I could be at a dance and I was dreaming all night how I thought I could hear the fiddle and fiddler say promenade all.

Priest's parents and schoolmaster suspected that Andrew and Emily knew the whereabouts of this, their favorite cousin, for the Smyths had received several pointed letters on the subject. If Andrew had helped Priest make his decision about going West, he did not seem to feel guilty. Neither he nor Emily told where the young man was.

They were both fond of young people and delighted in having them visit on the farm. Many of the letters that the Smyths enjoyed so much

[24] William Priest, Carson's Diggings, California, to "friend," July 20, 1851. AFS MSS.
[25] William Priest, Carson's Diggings, California, to Emily Allen Smyth, January 20, 1851. AFS MSS.

were from these youthful guests, like William Priest, who never forgot the hospitality extended to them. Other letters came from relatives in Alabama and Kentucky and, more and more as the years went by, from distant places within Texas. They got their mail at the Bevilport post-office. It was a pleasure for them to sit on the porch or before the fire and read long letters news-filled from outside their locale; the mail was the only means that they had of keeping up with people who had gone away from Jasper County.

IV

April 2, 1854, Andrew Constantine Smyth was born, the sixth child, the second son. Nancy, the oldest child, was nearing her eighth birthday; Susan was six; Araminta, called Minty, was four; George was three; and Frances was one. The youngest child was nicknamed Buddy. Nancy had already entered Indian Creek School, where Elisha Seale was teaching scholars from ages six to eighteen in one room.

Andrew talked seriously of opening a store at Bevilport and William A. Ferguson was interested in establishing a partnership with him. The county was experiencing a building boom, which had its good effect upon the sawmill by keeping the mill in almost continual operation.[26] So frequent were the orders for lumber that Andrew had to obtain rights to cut timber off other men's land in an effort to fill them.

At home, under Emily's direction, an orchard was planted across the road from the house, and crops of sugar cane, corn, and cotton were planted on a small scale. A little sugar mill was erected behind the house. Powered by mules, the mill produced syrup from the sugar cane. Peacocks paraded about the yard, giving an amusing contrast to the unpainted plainness of the house, and many kinds of farm animals idled in the lots near the barn.[27] China trees had developed well in the backyard and wild myrtle had been cultivated; since dogs must be kept, the myrtles, which would ward fleas away from the residence, were desirable. Countless details demanded attention. A little prosperity, it seemed, merely increased one's responsibilities.

In 1855 Andrew and Emily became aware that Jim, the new slave, had disappeared.[28] A day's search yielded nothing, nor did a week's,

[26] Account books and papers from the sawmill, 1852–1857. AFS MSS.
[27] Mention of the sugar mill, the peacocks, and the crops appears in the account books of the 1850's. AFS MSS.
[28] Andrew F. Smyth to M. Constantine Smyth, evidently a first draft of a letter dated at Jasper, 1855. AFS MSS.

nor a month's. Jim was gone. Writing to Conse in Mooresville, Alabama, a town not far from Moulton, Andrew asked that his brother inquire and advertise for the runaway. Conse, who was a clerk in a Mooresville store, wrote back:[29]

I must inform you of my failure to get your boy Jim. I went to Indiana & found the place where he had been in jail. When I got there of course I apprehended no danger from any source except the abolitionists, but upon inquiry of the jailor I found that he had broken jail and gone. Now whether he really broke jail I cannot determine. Then the question arose what was the best policy, and all I could do was advertise him in the St. Louis Republican and offered a reward of One hundred and fifty dollars to be delivered to any jail on the Missouri side of the Mississippi River, and I have not heard anything from there since. . . . no one regrets your loss more than I do.

As it had happened, said Conse, Jim had allied himself with some abolitionists "whose daily occupation was to cheat and defraud every man who placed himself within their reach." Jim was caught stealing money from one of the abolitionists and was jailed. Breaking jail, he was recaptured at once. When Jim's lawyer wrote Conse, he advised that the Smyths pay the bond and bring Jim back to Texas. But at that there was no assurance that passage for the Negro was safe.[30]

Evidently Andrew withdrew from the matter. Conse had made extravagant plans for returning Jim to Texas; Conse always made magnificent plans. Andrew disregarded the loss and credited it to experience. Never again did he want to purchase a slave. Ann was enough.

During the day Andrew was occupied with business. When the river was not low he might take a flatboat to Sabine Pass to be gone several weeks or sometimes well over a month. Stops along the river were more frequent—Town Bluff, Wiess's Bluff, Beaumont, and a number of new landings had grown in these ten or so years that Andrew had used the river. He still loved the water and made the trip downriver whenever he felt that the mill could spare him. More cotton than ever before was available because the worm had disappeared for a while, and finer things were to be had in the Sabine Pass and Galveston stores. Occasional steamboat trips to Bevilport had kept the stores there better supplied than the *Jasper* did. The routine of the trips had changed little, but it would be

[29] M. Constantine Smyth, Mooresville, Alabama, to Andrew F. Smyth, November 4, 1855. AFS MSS.

[30] M. Constantine Smyth, Mooresville, Alabama, to Andrew F. Smyth, November 19, 1855. AFS MSS.

wrong to say that they were monotonous, for new experiences were to be had each time.

When Andrew reached home Emily would prepare a tempting table. A visitor described one of those meals, "There was venison in abundance, fried squirrel as it never since has been cooked, fresh pork sausage and backbone, hot buttered biscuits with ribbon cane syrup or wild honey, sliced sweet potato pie and many other good things."[31]

Before a roaring fire, Andrew peeled sugar cane for the children to chew and perhaps he and Emily discussed all that had been, was being, and would be. The Smyths were planning every second what they might do next to better themselves. They felt a little older, maybe, but there was no stopping. The future was before them and Andrew's dreams were big.

[31] George Van Horn Moseley (ed.), *The Memoirs of George W. Armstrong*, pp. 50–51.

9. For East Texas the 1850's were years of progress in business. Some farmers were experiencing good times, the likes of which they had not seen before. This was the general picture. Of course, there were exceptions, such as a certain native of Georgia who did not find Texas an Eden: "The lofty expectations with which I started for this land of promise have withered & naught is left. . . . Again are all my fondest hopes scattered like autumn leaves before wind."[1]

I

In many cases towns grew rich with new residents and economic activity. Business opportunity, in fact, seemed available in all parts of the state. Galveston had risen conspicuously among American seaports, its variety of imports and exports supplying not only Texas but other places in the United States and foreign countries as well. The cruder aspects of frontier life had moved to the hot, barren prairies of West Texas, where in a lawless and struggling civilization the cattle empire was being born. Jasper County had emerged from the early years a substantial, well-settled, and, generally speaking, prosperous area. Broadcloth suits and silk dresses were not uncommon sights in the streets of Jasper and Bevilport; a surprising number of porches had become piazzas in these good years of the fifties.

Since there was more money to be spent in the county, Andrew decided late in 1855 to build a store in Bevilport.[2]

R. C. Doom, Mr. Lanier, Lewis Seale, and several others already had stores there, but room for more could be found. As Andrew was no longer in debt his income, less expenses, was clear profit. The mill had good and bad times, depending upon the demand for lumber, but in the past five years Andrew had found little to complain of. When the river was high enough, profitable trips had been made to Sabine Pass—trips which would be repeated, for cotton was now shipping at one dollar and a quarter per bale.[3]

[1] Frank J. West, unaddressed letter, Texas, ca. 1855. Frank J. West MSS.

[2] Andrew F. Smyth, Jasper County (?), to M. Constantine Smyth, 1855. AFS MSS.

[3] Andrew F. Smyth account book, 1855–1856. AFS MSS.

While the proposed store was in the planning stage Andrew discussed the matter with William A. Ferguson, who had joined in partnership with C. F. Alexander, the Sabine Pass merchant he had dealt with for several years. Ferguson and Alexander probably realized that eastern wholesale houses often sent a lesser quality of goods to Texas merchants; goods which were out of style elsewhere or were warehouse overflow. Texans did not seem to know the difference. But the partners figured that if first-grade goods were ordered by a Texas merchant in person, top quality could be assured, and the store, stocked in such a manner, would have so many customers that some would have to be turned away.

When Andrew told Ferguson his plans for a store in Bevilport, Ferguson was delighted. Ferguson outlined his and Alexander's plans for stocking the Sabine Pass store, offering to take Andrew in as a third partner. Andrew liked the idea but quickly admitted that he did not have the large amount of ready cash to invest.

Not one to lose a good prospect, Ferguson suggested that Andrew go ahead and build the store. In the finished building, the partnership of Alexander and Ferguson would place a modest supply of its own goods for sale.[4] Andrew's part would be to simply supply the store building in a good location. One afternoon, after a meal at Andrew's house, the matter was agreed upon.

Ferguson, with letters of credit from Galveston business houses, set out on the buying trip.[5] Early in July he was in New Orleans, where he bought some goods and waited for a New York sailing ship. Writing Andrew from New Orleans he said, "My impression is that I shall buy a good large stock for Bevilport as I believe it is the only thing to controll the trade at that point."[6] As his trip progressed, Ferguson became more excited at the thought of the riches that this endeavor might yield. July 25 he found a paradise of things to buy in New York City. In a quick note to Andrew his anxiety was evident: ". . . I think of buying a good stock, better than has ever been in Jasper County. You must roof up that house, we must get the goods open in September so as to furnish the fawl trade you may say to our friends to hold on as we can and will sell goods cheaper than any one else."[7]

[4] William A. Ferguson, Sabine Pass, Texas, to Andrew F. Smyth, January 18, 1856. AFS MSS.
[5] William A. Ferguson, New Orleans, Louisiana, to Andrew F. Smyth, July 12, 1856. AFS MSS.
[6] *Ibid.*
[7] William A. Ferguson, New York, New York, to Andrew F. Smyth, July 25, 1856. AFS MSS.

Andrew, however, did not begin the store until the next month. It was built beside the hotel in Bevilport and was a two-story structure with a low front porch and plank doors, the whole project costing a little over $250.[8] In October, Ferguson, at Sabine Pass, wrote Andrew that the New York goods had arrived. While the partners were working on a new store which they were opening in Beaumont on the Neches River, Ferguson forwarded a "very pretty stock" upriver to Andrew.[9] Alexander and Ferguson planned to come to Jasper soon and open another store; this store, they were sure, would "clean up the town of Jasper."[10] Sometime during October the goods arrived at Bevilport.

To Andrew's surprise, Ferguson's New York and New Orleans merchandise was not the usual calico, flour, or other items which found such ready buyers in the county. Opening the many cases and barrels, Andrew discovered hundreds of gallons of champagne, boxes of brandied cherries, numerous bottles of claret, rum, gin, and whiskey. Liquor was only one of the categories. Smiths' bellows in ridiculous quantity, anvils, barrels of mackerel, grindstones, bolts of silk and velvet, laces and satins, fancy household decorations—and still more—Ferguson was cutting his own throat.[11] People in Jasper County would have no use for half the items on the list. Why were they ordered in the first place?

Andrew probably felt rather sorry for the Sabine Pass partners, until he read the invoice supplied by the New York firms. The $7,000 worth of goods were billed to Ferguson and Smyth, Bevilport, Texas.

For a moment the invoice must have seemed like a death warrant. He remembered how freely Ferguson had referred to "we" in his letters. Grasping the situation, Andrew ordered the merchandise repacked and sent downriver to Ferguson and Alexander at Sabine Pass. Ferguson, still enthusiastic over future riches, shrugged his shoulders as he opened the goods and installed them in his Sabine Pass and Beaumont stores.[12]

The matter was closed for the time, and everyone agreed that a company named Ferguson and Smyth had never been. Andrew, happy to return to his sawmill and flatboats, locked the Bevilport store until a suitable arrangement could be made for its use.

[8] Andrew F. Smyth store building account, 1856. AFS MSS, Childers.

[9] William A. Ferguson, Sabine Pass, Texas, to Andrew F. Smyth, October 4, 1856. AFS MSS.

[10] Ibid.

[11] Bills from New York and New Orleans firms dated May through September, 1856. AFS MSS.

[12] William A. Ferguson, Jasper County, Texas, to Andrew F. Smyth, April 27, 1858. Notarized statement. AFS MSS.

II

In the summer of 1856 Texas newspapers carried reports of an internal-improvements bill, which had passed in the Texas Congress. The bill stipulated that when private subscription raised an amount not less than one thousand dollars for the improvement of some waterway, the state would give four times the amount toward the project. William Fields, state engineer, was one of George W. Smyth's close friends; and a year later, when George approached him with the idea of an improvement program on the Angelina and the Neches, Fields became interested.[13] As it was, steamboats could travel to Bevilport only when there was a rise in the river. Sunken logs, overhanging trees, stumps, sandbars, and clogs of refuse made river transportation hazardous and slow. When the water was high some of these dangers could be avoided.

George, having finished his term in Congress, was dividing his time between the Walnut Run farm and the General Land Office in Austin. He suggested the improvement idea to several of his friends in the county, and in a very short time a subscription program had been inaugurated.[14] The contract for the work would be given by the state engineer, who was to select the lowest bid from a series of estimates due at a date to be announced.

Andrew knew the rivers and decided that he would draw up an estimate. To organize this report would be time consuming, for it meant a thorough examination of the rivers during low water. Andrew did not need to hurry, because the state engineer had to check the rivers before he could accept bids. Without neglecting the mill or the flatboats, Andrew started on the river project at once.

III

In May, 1857, Andrew received bills from several New York mercantile houses for the goods which Ferguson had ordered. Writing Ferguson at Sabine Pass, he said, "I am sorry to know or even think that some steps had not been taken to quiet that matter . . . I now think I will come down to the pass before long perhaps next week . . . if it is necessary for me to do anything I want to do it soon."[15]

---

[13] William Fields, Houston, Texas, to George W. Smyth, June 7, 1857. AFS MSS.

[14] George W. Smyth, Jasper, Texas, to William Fields, August, 1857. AFS MSS.

[15] Andrew F. Smyth, Bevilport, Texas, to William A. Ferguson, June 9, 1857. AFS MSS.

Ferguson realized now that he had made foolish purchases. The store at Beaumont was closed and the one in Sabine Pass was obviously not to operate much longer. Laying the bills before Ferguson, Andrew insisted that the eastern companies be advised that there was no Ferguson and Smyth and that the debts belonged to Ferguson and Alexander alone. The debts were due, however, and Ferguson was not nearly so amiable as he had once been. Andrew, he said, had agreed to handle the merchandise, so he must help "settle up the business."[16] The whole idea was absurd, but Andrew's hands were tied.

He soon learned that the debts accumulated by Ferguson in New York, alone, amounted to $12,000, of which Alexander and Ferguson were responsible for three fourths, leaving Andrew with $3,000 to pay. Fortunately, Andrew was excluded from the New Orleans debts.[17] Andrew envisioned his home and his land being sold on the courthouse square and decided that at all costs such disgrace would be avoided.[18] At any rate, he had time to think it all over, because the New York houses would not press the matter before winter. More bills came in as the months passed. Finally, they were all there, and together they totaled $12,000, just as Alexander and Ferguson had said.

IV

The duty of the state engineer was to examine the rivers before the contract for improvement could be let. Because Mr. Fields, seriously ill, was unable to do this Andrew was hired to take his place.[19]

Beginning in the winter of 1858, Andrew and several workers went about thirty miles up the Angelina beyond Smyth's Landing and moved slowly downriver past the town and into the Neches. Obstructions in the rivers were placed in three classes, three varying degrees of danger to shipping. Log clogs immediately beneath the surface of the water were the worst hazards, and treacherous snags were considered almost as bad.[20] Andrew's reports indicated that the rivers were in dire need of improvement, as, of course, the subscribers to the project already knew.

16 William A. Ferguson, Jasper, Texas, to Andrew F. Smyth, June 20, 1857. AFS MSS.

17 William A. Ferguson, Jasper County, Texas, to Andrew F. Smyth, April 27, 1858. Notarized statement. AFS MSS.

18 Andrew F. Smyth, Bevilport, Texas, to D. Ayers, June 27, 1858. AFS MSS.

19 Andrew F. Smyth, Smyth's Landing, Texas, to William Fields, September 2, 1858. AFS MSS.

20 Notes on the river examination, 1858. AFS MSS.

Having submitted the report in August, 1858, Andrew was ready to prepare his estimate. Mr. Fields urged him to complete the estimate as soon as possible and to apply for the position of subengineer, in which capacity he would approve the contractor's work rather than directing the workmen himself.[21] As William Fields died in September, the estimate and application were submitted to E. F. Gray, the new state engineer.

Almost $3,000 had been raised by private subscription for the river project. The addition of state funds would make possible an extensive program.[22] Because of the change to a new state engineer, the appointments of contractor and subengineer were delayed for about a year.

V

The District Court of the United States, sitting at Galveston, ordered Andrew, Ferguson, and Alexander to appear before it in early December, 1858.[23] Eight business houses from New York and one in New Orleans had filed suits for the amounts owed and the costs of the trials.

Andrew was, as he stated in a letter to George, very busy with his flatboats and sawmill, but he was anxious to learn exactly where he stood in the matter with Ferguson. And he immediately took the situation in hand.

Ferguson asked the court that the suit be postponed until the next year and his request was granted.[24] In Jasper on January 10 he signed a paper saying that Andrew was not his business partner and that the firm of Ferguson and Smyth had never existed.[25] Ferguson reluctantly deeded his Sabine Pass land to Andrew, claiming that it was worth well over $3,000. The value of the property did not fully balance the debt, but at least Andrew did not have to go to court. Having obtained Ferguson's statement, Andrew sent notarized copies to each of the business houses implicated in his part of the debt. The documents were accompanied by a form letter:[26]

[21] William Fields, Hempstead, Texas, to Andrew F. Smyth, September 5, 1858. AFS MSS.

[22] Andrew F. Smyth account book, 1856–1861. AFS MSS.

[23] United States District Court, Galveston, Texas, to Andrew F. Smyth, Charles Alexander and William A. Ferguson, October 15, 1857. AFS MSS.

[24] Andrew F. Smyth, Bevilport, Texas, to H. N. and M. N. Potter, August 15, 1858. AFS MSS.

[25] William A. Ferguson, Jasper County, Texas, to Andrew F. Smyth, January 10, 1859. Notarized statement. AFS MSS.

[26] Andrew F. Smyth, Bevilport, Texas, to Betts, Nichols, and Company, *et al.*, June 11, 1859. AFS MSS.

You are doubtless surprised at the fact that Mr. Ferguson leaves a part of the debts of *Ferguson & Smyth* unpaid and makes no provision for their payment. I can assure you that it is an unpleasant thought for me seeing what little I have made through life sacrificed under the hammer to pay intrinsically another man's debts. I cannot get anything from him except property at a high price which is not available at present . . . if the parties will all agree to let the matter rest as it now is and permit me to sell the property and apply the proceeds exclusively to the payment of these debts, I will be able to satisfy this obligation.

The merchants speedily replied, willing to make arrangements. A few months of correspondence resulted in a two-year extension of Andrew's part of the debt. Galveston and Sabine Pass businessmen had given Andrew excellent recommendations and had explained the situation. The eastern companies were delighted with the "spirit" displayed by Andrew, considering that he had been placed in a "peculiar position."[27]

By selling the property in Sabine Pass, Andrew reduced the debt to $1,492.36.[28] Although the debt looked very large, ruin would not come to him as he had expected a short time before. But he was glad not to be in the shoes of Alexander and Ferguson, a mercantile firm which incidentally would never again enter the business life of Andrew F. Smyth.

VI

Through the months of 1859 and into 1860 Andrew finished and sold more lumber than he had sold in over five years.[29] Many new houses were being built in the Bevilport vicinity, some of them showing such fine touches as plaster walls and blue-tinted glass transoms. The Smyths were finding their two rooms too small for themselves and six children.

By Christmas, 1859, they had made rooms from the back porch and had replaced the log kitchen in the yard with a kitchen and dining-room ell connected to the back of the house by a breezeway.[30] From a Beaumont cabinetmaker Andrew ordered four high-post beds, two of black gum, two of beech.[31] Hide-bottom chairs were made at the mill and the

27 Reid, Tracy, and Company, New York, New York, to Andrew F. Smyth, June 29, 1859. AFS MSS.

28 Allen, McLean, and Bulkley, New York, New York, to Andrew F. Smyth, July 2, 1859. AFS MSS.

29 Andrew F. Smyth account book, 1859–1860. AFS MSS.

30 Architectural evidence in existing house; Andrew F. Smyth account books, 1859–1860. AFS MSS.

31 John Iscson, Beaumont, Texas, to Andrew F. Smyth, April 12, 1859. AFS MSS.

pineapple motif, first used on the gateposts, was maintained on the homemade furniture within the house.

When the weather permitted, life centered on the porch and in the entry, where a variety of comfortable chairs, a few tables, and the loom and spinning wheel were kept. Only on cold days did the family sit indoors where the fireplaces were, for the porch was well protected from rain and sun.

The flatboat business was still good although the steamboat's success on the Angelina and the Neches could be felt. At his river landing Andrew built a 125-foot steamer, the *Neches,* for a group of Jasper businessmen. The machinery for the boat was brought from Galveston.[32] Through supplying lumber and sending flatboats downriver, and with special projects such as building the *Neches,* Andrew was fast melting his debts to the New York merchants. The unused store in Bevilport stood closed and locked.

On June 1, 1860, Andrew was appointed subengineer of the Neches-Angelina improvement project by Governor Sam Houston.[33] W. M. Neyland, having submitted the lowest bid, had been appointed contractor in the year before.[34] Subengineer in more flowery terms meant assistant to the state engineer, with the responsibility of seeing that the contractor completed the job properly. For Andrew this position was most desirable in that he would need no assistants and would have time to attend to his interests at home. Neyland had already accomplished some of the river improvement, using a dredging mechanism operated by a team of Negroes. Additional private subscription had made possible the expansion of the original plans.

Working through the summer and fall, Neyland and his workers pulled snags from the dark water and widened the rivers wherever necessary to eliminate sharp turns. Andrew observed, suggested, and generally criticized in notes to Mr. Neyland. December 20 Andrew wrote the authorities in Austin that the project "as agreed upon" was complete, sending a bill for his services with the letter.[35] Neyland was paid $18,161.25 for his year and a half of work and Andrew received $5,200.-

[32] Copy of a contract between Andrew F. Smyth, Z. Williams Eddy, and S. S. Adams for building the steamer *Neches,* Jasper County, Texas, December 29, 1859. AFS MSS.

[33] Sam Houston, Austin, Texas, to Andrew F. Smyth, June 1, 1860. AFS MSS.

[34] State of Texas, Harris County, Texas, to W. M. Neyland, July 4, 1859. AFS MSS.

[35] Andrew F. Smyth, Bevilport, Texas, to Sam Houston, December 20, 1860. AFS MSS.

00 for both his examination of the rivers under Mr. Fields and his job as
subengineer. To Andrew's pay was added 12 per cent advance pay for
"future examination of the river."[36] His affairs with the New York business houses were closed early in the next year.[37]

VII

When the Texas Democratic Convention met at Galveston in the spring
of 1860 it adopted resolutions declaring the right of a state to secede
from the United States. Texas, it said, would secede if an abolitionist
Republican was elected President in the coming election. The idea of
secession for Texas was not new in the year 1860; since Texas had lost
territorial claims in the Texas and New Mexico Act of 1850, some land-
hungry people within the state had been bitter and had spoken of secession. To the National Democratic Convention this 1860 assembly at
Galveston sent proslavery delegates. When Abraham Lincoln won the
presidency over the Democratic candidate, Texas proslavery men hurried a secession movement inside the state. Governor Houston spoke
vehemently against the secessionists. Because he realized what would
happen, he refused to call the legislature for the special session which
the secessionists requested.

At the fourth of July celebration in Jasper, George W. Smyth was invited to speak on the subject of secession. He prepared and delivered a
very long speech, which began with the slavery question and traced it
from its origin to its present effect upon the people of Jasper County and
East Texas that hot July of 1860. Meticulous, barely biased, the speech
gave both sides of the secession question, elaborated with quotations,
anecdotes, and the like. George had come from his sporadic convales-
cence to make the speech, vowing that it would be his last official word
in the county on the topic. People from as far away as Nacogdoches had
appeared at the celebration for the express purpose of hearing the
speech. With great physical effort George informed his neighbors and
visitors of the finer political points involved in the problem.[38]

Sitting at a picnic on the ground with Andrew and Emily and Frances, George could be quite candid in stating his disapproval of secession.
But he knew that most of his audience did not agree with him. The very
spirit of the day was proof enough of that.

[36] *Ibid.*
[37] Receipts dated January and February, 1861. AFS MSS.
[38] *The East Texas Clarion*, Jasper, Texas, Saturday, July 21, 1860. Vol. I,
No. 36.

In communities, counties, and towns all over Texas meetings were held and memorials sent to the Governor pleading that the legislature be called. Soon enough the people of Andrew's part of Jasper County had just such a meeting.

A crowd filled the Indian Creek Church on an evening late in fall. As in most meetings of that kind, a few spoke while the rest listened, contented with their voting power, almost hidden in the cigar smoke. During the course of the meeting, Lewis Seale rose to speak in behalf of himself, his father, and his family. To secede would undoubtedly mean war, he said, which in turn would mean the defeat of the South, the ruin of Texas. Nothing, he said, would survive. If this was apparent, why couldn't the slaves be freed by their owners? Each planter might give his slaves freedom, a small number of farm animals, and some acres of good land—all with the understanding that the slaves would pay for these things over a period of years; the white man, then, would be able to control the liberated Negro. Texas should definitely remain in the Union. If the slavery friction was settled within the South, there would be no need for secession. Otherwise, Texas and the whole South would surely be swept by Negroes, freed by war, who, when they did not starve on the road, would be an unremitting danger to the white man. In conclusion, Lewis announced that he and his father would be the first to follow this freedom policy if it was adopted. Jasper County, he said, could at least try the plan, for it would help ward off the unavoidable trouble to come.[39]

The chairman of the meeting—reputed to have been George W. Smyth—probably had a difficult time keeping the hall quiet during Lewis' speech; but when the speaker sat down, the sarcasms, laughter, and thinly veiled insults began, and lasted intermittently until the adjournment. When the talking was over, the Indian Creek assembly sent a memorial to the Governor asking that the legislature be called. As for Lewis Seale, he returned home that night and sold everything he owned to his son Elias for the $30,000 in gold which Elias had reaped from the rush to California.[40]

Despite the many resolutions received, Sam Houston refused to call the legislature. Certainly, others agreed that secession was wrong. George W. Smyth, the owner of twenty-eight slaves, agreed with Hous-

[39] Told to William Seale, Sr., by Emily Allen Smyth. Told to author in a conversation in August, 1961.
[40] *The Sunday Enterprise,* Beaumont, Texas, November 27, 1932, p. 8–A (clipping).

ton in this matter and wrote the Governor offering his assistance. Andrew's opinion seems to have been somewhere between the two extremes. But Houston's followers were scattered and ineffective. Finally, the secession leaders in Texas called a convention to meet in Austin late in January, 1861. Houston, in desperation, summoned the legislature, which somewhat softened the radicals' blow by requiring that the issue of secession be submitted to a vote of the people. On February 23, 1861, an overwhelming majority of Texans voted to secede from the Union. During March, Texas joined the Confederacy.

Standing fast in his opposition to both acts, Sam Houston was removed from office, to return heartbroken to his family. Earlier, the Federal commander of the state had surrendered 2,500 men and the United States military installations in Texas to a representative of the secession convention.

VIII

Andrew was not as concerned over politics as his brother, but he was opposed to secession, probably because he respected George's viewpoint. It seemed to him that the differences of the North and the South could be handled within the framework of the United States government, avoiding the inevitable destruction that war would bring. The South, he thought, was correct in principle but foolish and wasteful to carry it so far beyond what he considered the bounds of reason.

Andrew had very little to gain by a Southern victory. While his business depended upon the agricultural prosperity of others, he could not see that the loss of a war would bring to an end the farmers' good times. Cotton and tobacco were giving way to the big-scale lumber industry before the very eyes of the planters, and often certain spots in the river were jammed with logs to such a degree that a flatboat could not move on but had to wait until the lumbermen were out of the way. Weeks were required to float logs to downriver sawmill sites. Andrew could envision a time when this lumber trade would be a real problem to rivermen.[41] It was a problem to the farmers, too, in that the entire lumber industry was a threat to the existence of the plantations, war or no war.

With so much to be done, Andrew was impatient with the war, far less so, however, than George, who fell into a prolonged state of depres-

[41] George W. Smyth, Walnut Run, Jasper County, Texas, to Andrew F. Smyth, October 5, 1860. AFS MSS.

sion, spending hours in his parlor writing somber letters and poems.[42] Andrew did not brood and would not have even had he shared George's interest in public matters. His reaction to problems was, as it had been in the William Ferguson affair, to do the best he could with what was before him. When and if the Civil War came to his door or to his friends' doors, he would become involved.

All that Andrew and Emily had worked for had been seriously endangered during the recent business crisis. They had realized the danger only too well at the time. The world which they created for themselves, even though not the summit of their visions, was so comfortable, so perfectly attuned to what they enjoyed, that the thought of losing it had not occurred to them.

Then, in the midst of their constant talk of better things, had come the realization that what they had now could be taken away, quickly, legally, leaving them with nothing. The winter, spring, and summer of 1859, before terms had been reached with Ferguson, had been hard on the Smyths: eight mercantile houses in New York and New Orleans had made threats by mail, then in person through Galveston lawyers, to lay hold of everything they owned. Rather than thinking of what they now had as a foundation for something more, Andrew and Emily came to love their plain farm as home, a thing to protect. Thoughts of moving from the land they had cleared, the house they had built, and the friends they had made droned through their minds and tormented them. As if to make every second count, they had remodeled their house, trying to forget that it could be taken away from them at any moment. They talked and they worried.

Finally, on a midsummer flatboat trip, Andrew sought Ferguson out in Sabine Pass and brought him back to Jasper, there to settle the problem once and for all. In a quick, effective fit of rage he demanded compensation from his supposed partner. A persistent trader might have made more agreeable arrangements but with the stakes so high Andrew was happy to have the debt reduced to a figure that he could pay. Ferguson played fast games; that a chance to win was counterbalanced with the chance to lose was a fact of life he recognized. Of both he partook freely. Andrew was not a speculator in that sense and he was quite willing to pay money he did not really owe, under these particular cir-

[42] Frances G. Smyth, Walnut Run, Jasper County, Texas, to Emily Smyth, July 20, 1862. AFS MSS.

cumstances, to preserve all that he had accumulated. It was a practical outlook even if the idea infuriated him. When the eastern companies agreed to his proposal to pay the certain amount Andrew set himself to satisfying the debt, glad at last to be rid of the matter.

The difficult months of 1859 opened Andrew's and Emily's eyes to realities which they had not seen before. Obscured by their ambition and untiring dedication to work, the things that they really wanted had fallen under foot in a chase toward a phantom goal, which teased them so at each plateau that they could look only ahead, almost oblivious to what was around them.

Presented with the possibility of losing what they had, they began to sense the importance of where they were and what they had made for themselves so far. This pleasant life could not really be elevated by further material advances, though that is what they had worked toward for years and it was in their natures to work still more. Not for a moment had they been unhappy; but at the same time they had never stopped and known that they were happy. The experience of 1859 had awakened them.

As established citizens of Texas in these Confederate States of America, Andrew and Emily approached the future with uncertainty. The fields and woods and buildings within a mile of their porch belonged to them. They no longer had debts to meet. As always, they had plans for expanding their business and home but they wondered what the war between the states would bring to these woods. Surely, it would not take away all the dear possessions which they had so recently come to appreciate.

PART THREE

Riverman

10. It has been estimated that one third of the people of Texas were against secession. This opposition did not organize into a party, and state politics were dominated by those in favor of the Southern cause. The citizens who were against the political current reacted in different ways: some fled to Mexico, some joined the Union forces, but the great majority stayed at home, giving the Confederacy half-hearted support.

I

Andrew and George were among this majority. If Andrew's views might have harmed his standing in the community, George would have ruined a good political career by taking the platform against war. The brothers were not wanting to sacrifice all that they had worked for.[1]

Nancy, Andrew's fifteen-year-old daughter, had been attending school in the Indian Creek Church. Her teacher, Elisha Seale, proposed to her at the end of the spring term in 1860. Elisha selected an afternoon in May to call upon Andrew and Emily and discuss the proposal of marriage.

While he sat on the front porch talking with the family, he noticed a deer walking from the mill road. Abruptly, he jumped over the railing, ran to the deer, which made no effort to flee, and cut its throat. Carrying the carcass proudly on his shoulders to the house, he met a file of sad faces, which surprised him somewhat, since he thought that they had been cheering only moments before. The cheers had been protests and had lasted only an instant, for the Smyths realized what was happening after it was too late. The deer was Araminta's pet, found as a fawn and raised there in the yard. Minty could not be consoled at all, even by the almost tearful apologies of the school teacher. Andrew, Emily, and Nancy understood the mistake, and the visit continued and slowly relaxed.

It was no happy thought for Andrew to surrender a daughter so young though he knew that there were younger marriages from time to time in the county. Still, Nancy had never seemed much like a child. Serious about everything and fond of duty in the same way that her mother was,

[1] M. Constantine Smyth, Mooresville, Alabama, to Andrew F. Smyth, May 10, 1862. AFS MSS.

she was not as flippant as the other children, say, Minty, for example, who forgot about the deer in a few hours and went about her play. Nancy had loved her parents more than most children and it was hard for them to know that she wanted to marry.

Elisha, like his brother, Elias, had gone to the California gold fields ten years earlier, two weeks after William Priest had left. Elias amassed a fortune in gold, but Elisha, not so lucky, had found himself operating a San Francisco tollgate in an effort to make money for the clipper-ship passage home. Most brothers would have felt a certain obligation to help one another. But not these two, who had been reared in the house of tough-crusted Lewis Seale. When he first reached California, Elisha spent too much time living the wild life to suit his brother. And for him to end up without any money seemed about what he deserved. It had been a good lesson.

Back in Jasper County, Elisha became a schoolmaster and a familiar face on Sunday at the Indian Creek Church. He lacked the financial abilities of his father but he had some knowledge of Latin, Greek, and the sciences; and his religious interests did not escape the observation of Emily. If his fascination with experimental farming did not make him rich, he at least had his school teaching to supplement his income. Satisfied with the match but not convinced that their daugher was old enough, the Smyths gave a reluctant consent. Preparations were made for the wedding, which occurred late in May, 1861, at the Smyths' house.

For the remainder of 1861 war seems to have had little effect upon the lives of Andrew and Emily. Business continued as usual and the household was operated as before. Soldiers of Texas were on the frontier and in the New Mexico territory fighting Indians and Federal troops, alternately. Now and again a local boy ran away from home to join the army, but had it not been for its domination of conversation the war might have passed unnoticed in Jasper County.

There was, however, some concern over relatives who lived in the older Southern states, less isolated from the action than Texas. Regarding the war, Conse wrote from Alabama to his brother:[2]

It is utterly unnecessary for me to say anything in regard to the political trouble of our Country, But that we are in the midst of a revolution "however unholy and unconstitutional it may be," has no parallel in the history of this or any Other Country, Cannot be denied by any intelligent man. The causes which brought this war upon our once happy and united country are evident to every

[2] M. Constantine Smyth, Mooresville, Alabama, to Andrew F. Smyth, August 10, 1861. AFS MSS.

thinking mind. I was for the *Union* until every proposition for an amicable adjustment of the pending difficulties between the two Sections of the Country were hurled from the Federal Congress and treated with profound Contempt. Then I raised my feeble voice in the defense of Alabama, my native State.

Andrew might have been surprised at his brother's noble spirit, had he read no farther.[3]

When the question necessarily comes up, have you Volunteered your services to fight the battles of your Country against Mr. Lincoln and his abolition hosts, I answer no, because Circumstances thus far have prevented, but I hope these obstacles will soon be removed, and that I will be found battling for our independence and our Constitutional rights . . . we should feel thankful to the great Creator of all things for his omnipotent goodness and mercy in this our trying time without which we could not have survived our political troubles in Consequence of Mr. Lincoln's Blockade . . . I think I will visit you in the fall as I will have no business of any importance to attend to.

He was the same old Conse, not changed at all.

George had not approved of secession and, off the political scene entirely, he spent his time managing affairs at his Walnut Run farm. He suffered from ill-health, which was in no way improved by his son's talk of joining the army. To amuse himself, George still wrote poetry and he now had ample time, for his part in overseeing the farm usually included little more than listening to the reports of Uncle January. One of the poems that he wrote concerning the war was "The Ranger Boy and the Musical Coon," a copy of which he wrote in ink and sent to Andrew:[4]

> It matters not how serious or solemn we may be,
> It is diverting truly friends at Indian Creek to see,
> A regular attendant there, an old deceitful coon,
> A raising on his tiptoes high, and reaching for a tune,
>
> Though fond of music seemingly, it is beyond his reach,
> He cannot get the hang of it, much less, he couldn't teach,
> When'er occasion comes to sing, in rising, has no doubt,
> With folded arms he wrings and screws but cannot get it out,
>
> Perhaps dear reader you would like, before I further go,
> The author of these few remarks in poetry to know,
> I, by my honest labor live, within the lone star state,
> Reared up in the far western wiles, in quite an early date,

---

[3] *Ibid.*

[4] Another of the six poems by George W. Smyth found in the steamer trunk. AFS MSS.

I had a good old father then that lived by raising stock,
And this poor ranger boy, my friend, would herd his sheep in flock,
I long remained in early life unlettered and unlearned,
And by this calling I persued a scanty pittance earned,

All things worked smoothly on until this wretched war began,
We volunteered all round about, till scarce was left a man,
In much confusion all were soon from their dear loved ones torn,
To travel o'er far distant lands, in regions yet unknown,

We've traveled through the eastern states for 18 months or more,
And day by day, sore trials met, and oft in battle soar,
I'm far away from home sweet home, and hills and valleys intervene,
May angels kind their vigils keep and from impending danger screen,

Although in camps we suffer much, and have but little time,
That little this poor ranger boy devotes to scribbling rhyme,
The preachers here do often say our talents should not die,
I therefore feel this gift of mine shall never dormant lie,

I've been upon the battlefield where blood in torrents run,
Where glittering spears and pointed steel, more dazzling than the sun,
I've heard the thundering cannon sound, to monkey shows have been,
In camps I've learned a few small tricks, but still I'm awful green,

But now before I further stray I think I shall return,
To my old friend who has for years such sainted aspect worn,
If gifted with the organ tune it surely must lie deep,
For fifty years he's tried most tunes and cannot one tune keep,

He cannot sing tis all in vain, so further trial stay,
He can as well the sun command with all its brilliant rays,
Or reach on tiptoes with his arm the orbit of the moon,
As ever to successful be in singing the perfect tune.

George W. Smyth sent rhymes and notes to his brother throughout
the war. Andrew did not fail to notice George's poor health and the
growing bitterness that he felt about the war. The visits between the
brothers became more numerous than they had been when both were
occupied with business.

Infrequent letters kept Andrew and Emily advised of conditions in
Alabama and Kentucky. Captain Smyth had died in 1856 after having
been bedridden for two years. Nancy Allen died very suddenly in the
fall of 1860, to be followed by Benjamin in the next summer. Of the
close relatives, therefore, only several brothers and sisters remained.
News of deaths and births always came abruptly in letters, but then letters had been the only connection with home in years. Time and the loss

of loved ones had made Texas home. As the severance from Alabama and Kentucky became more pronounced, the flow of letters diminished.

In February, 1862, Elias Seale began organizing a company which would march from Jasper County to join the Texas Cavalry. Seeing his neighbors join the company, Andrew decided to take an active part in the war, which suddenly seemed close to where he was. He volunteered for twelve months' service and was made a first lieutenant. When required to state his occupation Andrew said "farmer."[5]

The company was still forming when George W. Smyth's son said that he wanted to join. George gave his approval. The younger Smyth was eighteen and his father was afraid that discouragement would cause him to run away and join another company; young people were so obstreperous.

During mid-March the company left Bevilport, crossed the Angelina, and moved west.

Emily and the children were by no means alone while Andrew was away. Besides Ann and her two little sons, five locally hired slaves and a white overseer were at the mill, all of whom had cabins within calling distance of the house. Since Jerry Delaney and Mr. Holland had also left for war, Emily felt uncomfortable around the workers, but each day food was taken across the road and set out in the employees' dining room, a crude frame building which Andrew had put up in 1855. From the *Weekly Civilian & Gazette,* a Galveston newspaper to which the Smyths subscribed, Emily could keep more or less informed of the war situation.[6] In the third week of June she was surprised by Andrew's return home.

The Jasper company had been on its way to San Antonio, where it would become Company G 13th Texas Mounted Volunteers. When the men reached Crockett, Andrew said, they had been ordered to mobilize.[7] After that, May 25, Andrew and Mose Lee, the second lieutenant, were discharged. A recent conscription act exempted men over thirty-five from military service; Andrew was forty-five.[8] Within the time it had taken the company to march from Bevilport to Crockett and then a dis-

---

[5] Colonel John H. Burnett, 13th Texas Cavalry, to Andrew F. Smyth, May 25, 1862. Discharge from the Civil War. AFS MSS.

[6] *Weekly Civilian & Gazette,* Galveston, Texas, to Andrew F. Smithers (?), January 9, 1860. AFS MSS.

[7] *The Sunday Enterprise,* Beaumont, Texas, November 27, 1932, p. 8–A (clipping).

[8] Colonel John H. Burnett, 13th Texas Cavalry, to Andrew F. Smyth, May 25, 1862. Discharge from the Civil War. AFS MSS.

tance along the San Antonio Road, Andrew's credentials had been examined and his discharge was in the next dispatch from headquarters.

In early fall Yankee ships had moved into the Gulf of Mexico, and the Gulf coast was blockaded. The backwoods had to do the best it could with what was already upriver, for the supplies in coastal stores would soon be exhausted. Everyone knew that the Yankees had a keen eye for Galveston. It was even suggested that the city be burned to the ground so that it would be of no use to the invaders.[9] In October the city was surrendered intact. This must have been disturbing to the people upriver, yet they were very safe, living in a world seemingly isolated from the war. Galveston was recovered on New Year's Day, 1863.

Although the blockade was not gone, the great want for goods in the city that people had expected did not materialize. After a short period of idleness, clever blockade runners maintained a lively trade between themselves, Europe, and the West Indies.[10] From Galveston, goods could be rushed to places all over the South.

Elisha and Nancy had lived first with Andrew and Emily; then they moved to Lewis Seale's house. If Emily was partial to any one of her children, it was Nancy. In the short period that Elisha spent in the army Nancy lived at home; and when he returned to Jasper County in 1862 to teach school he and his wife visited the Smyths frequently. While Andrew was away Nancy refused to let her mother spend a night alone. Late in December, 1862, Nancy gave birth to a daughter whom Elisha named Emily.

During the following spring Andrew stopped sending flatboats downriver and reduced the mill's production drastically.[11] Perhaps for the first time in his career he really became a farmer. He had no other choice. Should Northern troops occupy Texas, Sabine Pass was the most likely point of entry; therefore, taking flatboats downriver involved danger. Very few customers appeared at the mill, except in special cases, such as the man downriver who wanted a ferry built and shipped to him.[12] People did not build houses, and in some instances women were the only members of a family left at home, with far more significant worries than house building. Business gradually came to a standstill. In the year

[9] Earl Wesley Fornell, *The Galveston Era: The Texas Crescent on the Eve of Secession*, p. 298.
[10] *Ibid.*
[11] S. Wiess, Wiess's Bluff, Texas, to Andrew F. Smyth, October 1, 1864; S. Wiess, Wiess's Bluff, Texas, to Andrew F. Smyth, December 12, 1864. AFS MSS.
[12] S. Wiess, Wiess's Bluff, Texas, to Andrew F. Smyth, 1864. AFS MSS.

1864 Andrew found that one homemade account book served him for the entire twelve months.

Twenty Federal gunboats with 5,000 men left New Orleans in September, bound for Sabine Pass. The object of the expedition was to capture Sabine Pass, placing the mouths of the Sabine and Neches in the hands of Federal troops, who would thereby control East Texas as well as a land route to Houston and Galveston. Beside the Pass was a lanky, crude system of earthworks manned by forty-two men and six cannon.

In command of the fort was First Lieutenant Dick Dowling, a twenty-five–year–old Irish immigrant. September 7 the gunboats reached their destination, ready to make short work of the fort and rush into Sabine Lake. During the following afternoon three gunboats moved toward the fort, intending to capture it before any soldiers were put ashore. Within a quick forty-five minutes Dick Dowling and his men, concentrating their fire on the boats one by one, put one of the gunboats out of commission, caused another to go aground, and finally had the surrender of all three. The Union commander in charge ordered the expedition back to New Orleans.

Knowing the Pass as well as he did, Andrew must have been very interested in Dowling's victory. It was a feeling strange indeed to realize that such a familiar place had been the scene of an exciting part of the war. Dick Dowling became a hero, celebrated in his own time, but it is doubtful that many people admired the Lieutenant more than did the East Texas backwoodsmen, oblivious of the lure of Galveston and Houston, who felt that he had kept the war from their doorsteps.

Early in the next year gunboats and an army headed for Texas by way of the Red River, traveling through Louisiana. Company G 13th Texas Mounted Volunteers—the Jasper Volunteers—were among those who met the Union General Banks at Mansfield, Louisiana, and, after two successful encounters, caused him to retreat.[13] Elias Seale, still in charge of the Jasper men, had been made major just prior to this.

The incidents at Sabine Pass and Mansfield, and the burning of the railroad depot at Beaumont were the closest that the Civil War ever came to Andrew and Emily. In the usually crowded account books is a conspicuous void for the war years of the 1860's. Here and there was a trifling matter to settle at the courthouse or perhaps an order for a small amount of lumber. To say that Andrew was inactive in business, though, is not to say that he was idle.

[13] *The Jasper Newsboy*, Jasper, Texas, March 22, 1962, Vol. 97, No. 38, p. 8.

The election for chief justice of the county was scheduled for the first day in August, 1864. Andrew was interested. Contacting friends in various parts of the county he launched what seems to have been a subtle campaign. Andrew's main opponent was Judge Goode, who had served in the office for several terms. When the election was over, Andrew was advised that he had won by a "large majority," which delighted him, proved by the fact that he took special precautions to preserve the letter.[14] In this new capacity he had been elected to a two-year term, during which he would try civil and criminal cases, as well as be a sort of mayor of the county.

The autumn after Andrew took office the Confederacy entered the months which would be its most difficult. Jasper County was still far removed from the scene of action, as was most of Texas. Yet, it was often a sleepless time for those who had fathers, husbands, or sons fighting somewhere a long way off; and just as sleepless were those who wondered what would become of themselves if the Southern cause was lost.

Nothing eventful occurred in Andrew's courtroom. Several disputes over heirship and guardianship needed his attention, but the courtroom life of Judge Smyth was unexciting.[15] He found, moreover, that not all his responsibilities were in court. In line with the apprehension of these hard months of the Confederacy, Valentine Wiess, who lived at Wiess's Bluff on the Neches, wrote Andrew:[16]

Allow me to introduce to you a matter which needs early attention. There is at this place about Thirty or Forty grown Negro men—apart of which are in my charge in the employ of the Gov'nt—And as you are well aware the Negroes at this time are not kept under strict discipline—on acct of so many of the citizens being in the army.—I have introduced the same subject to Judge Goode last year, when he was in Office—to send us an Order for a Patroll, which he promised me he would do but did not. I therefore hope that by furnishing you the names of the citizens & soldiers who are at present here on detail, that you will Immediately send us necessary papers for a Patroll—so that we may keep the Negroes in discipline,—or otherwise it may come to a bad end.

Andrew would have done well to issue the order if for no other reason than to give the people of Wiess's Bluff peace of mind. To "Smyth's Landing" were sent numerous notes of complaint—this village was without flour, that farmer needed salt. Advising Andrew that a certain ferry

14 Judge Goode, Jasper, Texas, to Andrew F. Smyth, August 1, 1864. AFS MSS.
15 Andrew F. Smyth papers as chief justice, 1864–1866. AFS MSS.
16 V. Wiess, Wiess's Bluff, Texas, to Andrew F. Smyth, February 20, 1865. AFS MSS.

had sunk, a citizen insinuated that the Judge should build another at his own expense for duty's sake.[17]

Hearing the complaints of his neighbors, George W. Smyth involved himself in Jasper County's wartime problems. He made no attempt to conceal his resentment that able youths were dying by the thousands in battle, nor that the war was still a foolish thing in principle. When in 1864 a number of slaves in the county were drafted to work on the Sabine Pass and Beaumont Railroad Line, to try to complete the tracks, which were nowhere near even a useful stage, George wrote to the authorities: "You impressed all our mules which you had no right to do. We only obeyed because you held the sword over our heads. Though only about half a crop has been made, we are giving our tythe of corn and meat to the army, while some among us actually suffer for the want of bread."[18]

George, like Andrew, gave cotton and corn to the army each year, for he felt a loyalty to Texas and to his son, who fought with the Jasper company.[19] But he referred to the war as the "rebellion" and wanted no part of it. His health became worse as his worries over the war and his son deepened. Andrew made more frequent trips to the house on Walnut Run than had ever been necessary, even when he was watching after the crops while George was away.

It was in the summer of 1865 that the Confederacy and the Confederate government in Texas finally collapsed. The last battle was won beside the Rio Grande by Southern troops who did not know that the war had already ended.

II

January 8, 1866, an election for delegates to the State Constitutional Convention was held. George was told that he had been nominated to represent Jasper County. On election day it was with great difficulty that he mounted his horse and headed to Jasper to look into the matter. A neighbor ran to the gate and called to George as he rode by, "Where are you going?"

"To town," George answered.

[17] N. L. Brown, Jasper, Texas, to Andrew F. Smyth, December 27, 1864. AFS MSS.

[18] George W. Smyth, Jasper, Texas, to George B. McGruder, July 20, 1864. GWS MSS, UTA.

[19] George W. Smyth, Jasper, Texas, to Z. Williams Eddy & Adams, November 28, 1861. GWS MSS, UTA.

"What is to be done in town today?"

"Nothing but the election."

"Who are the candidates?"

"I believe my friends are running my name as a candidate."

"In that case, I'll ride to town with you and vote for you."[20]

George won the election. It is possible that he rode to town not to vote but to withdraw his name. Frances was concerned over his health and none could deny that he looked sick, walking with a cane all the time, his hair recently gray, and his conversation wandering in a way so unlike him. But if Frances wanted him to stay at home, his neighbors' influence again was greater. He felt that they counted on him now as they had in years past and he refused to ignore their wishes. Also to be considered was his interest in the new constitution.

February 7 he sat uncomfortably at the opening meeting in Austin, fatigued by the stage ride, which had left him with a persistent cough. Heated debate between the Unionists and secessionists filled the following weeks. George attended each session religiously, remarking, in notes, that some of the ideas brought up were unacceptable. He said nothing in the meetings but expressed his ideas freely at dinner or on walks which he and other representatives took.

In the morning of the twenty-first, he was found dead in his hotel room. His kin in Jasper County had not received the news when the convention adjourned the next day to attend the funeral and then the burial in the State Cemetery in Austin.

III

Major Elias Seale returned home to find that his land had not been farmed nor cared for in the last two years of the war. His Negroes, including Uncle Dick, remained at home. Old Joshua had died and Elias was faced with having to support his parents, his younger brothers and sisters, and his wife and children. Elias' problem was not unique, for a great many men, especially those who had been to war, had returned to similar situations.

Perhaps Elisha and Nancy were having as easy a time as anyone. He had reopened the Indian Creek School and if he made no money he at least was paid in corn, sausage, woven cloth, and the like.[21]

[20] *Journal of the Texas Convention of 1866,* Vol. 4. Cited in Elbert Jefferson Myers, "Life of George W. Smyth," an unpublished MA thesis.

[21] Elisha D. Seale account book for 1866–1869. Elisha DeKalb Seale MSS.

Andrew, deeply hurt and feeling somewhat lost by the report of his brother's death, was made executor of the George W. Smyth estate. Letters written by fellow politicians had given the family the details of George's last hours. He had coughed continually while he was in Austin, and early in the morning of the twenty-first of February had fallen unconscious. The men with whom he shared the hotel room woke up and tried to render assistance, but to no avail. He died shortly before dawn; the convention had been shocked at the news.[22]

June 25, 1866, Andrew was elected to serve another two-year term as chief justice of the county. Enough of the paper work involved in settling George's vast estate had been done so that George, Jr., could handle things from then on.

It was sometime during 1866 that Lieutenant Colonel George Custer and a small company of men moved into Jasper to remain a short time. Andrew undoubtedly was the one to whom they addressed themselves. The soldiers caused no trouble and made a rather elegant appearance before the young ladies of Jasper.

A number of these belles one day decided that the local men were no fun. Therefore, why not entertain some of the Yankees at a ball? At the party the soldiers and the ladies were having a splendid time when a series of gunshots were fired into the hall. Glasses were smashed and people ran in all directions. Those who fired the shots left town as fast as they could. Racing along trails, through creeks, and in woods, they soon reached a riverbottom on either the Angelina or the Neches. It is known that one of the men hardly looked back until he was safely established in West Texas. Fortunately, the Union soldiers did not know the country too well or there might have been trouble.[23] From all accounts, the dancing resumed as though nothing had happened. How lucky it was for Andrew that the men escaped; had they been captured they would have been in his courtroom by morning, placing the chief justice in an uncomfortable position.

Some months later, pranksters shot holes in the soldiers' tents during a heavy rainstorm. Andrew was again saved from an unpleasantry when no one was arrested. But while the search was going on, he wondered if he had been wise to sign the Decree of Amnesty, which had restored his rights as an American citizen and permitted him to hold this job of judge.

---

[22] H. Stuart, Austin, Texas, to "The Family of the Hon. George W. Smyth," February 21, 1866. GWS MSS, UTA.

[23] Mrs. Charles Martin to author in a conversation, August 15, 1962, Kirbyville, Texas.

Stories of various kinds of reactions to the soldiers grew up everywhere. Some were true and some were not. Undoubtedly, the men who fired the shots into the dancing room of the hotel and into the tents had no intention to kill anyone. After all, as many friends of theirs were at the ball as were Yankees. They simply wanted to show the soldiers that they could and would fight a situation which displeased them, no matter if the entire United States Army was present. They resented the appearance of the soldiers, whom they considered personal enemies as well as men who were opposed to all that they loved. The incident at the hotel was the only hostile occurrence involving Jasper County people and Yankees in the whole postwar period. Mischief was played but it was usually directed at individuals or at outside groups, like the troops whose tents were shot. For the "foreigners" the populace of the community felt a hate which was by no means extraordinary. Although the war had taken place far from the county, fathers and sons had participated, and now to have the enemy flaunt its victory on the very streets of Jasper was more than an insult.

The resentment was inherited by the children, who reasoned that their heritage had been stolen from them by the war, or, more plainly, the Yankees. When times grew difficult for farmers and, consequently, the merchants, they looked to the life before the war as a glorious experience, taken away in its infancy, never to be reclaimed. For some, those days had indeed been better.

Besides his activities as judge, Andrew was working to build his business back to what it had been. In 1866 he took six flatboats to Sabine Pass and from there he made the usual trips to Galveston for goods to be shipped upriver aboard the *Pelican State*, the *Early Bird*, the *Rough and Ready*, or the *Sunflower*—packets which plied the Neches irregularly. By shipping cotton at two dollars per bale, Andrew realized about $900 from this endeavor.[24] He also did a considerable amount of surveying within the county, although this was a sideline.[25]

Somehow the mill never recovered from the war years. People did not have the money for building new houses and stores, and the steam mill was in the East Texas timberlands to stay. Small orders were filled each month for so many feet of cypress or pine but Andrew's mill was no longer a conspicuous factor in the income. The Bevilport store still stood locked and unused, even though the town had room for another store. Fairly regular steamboat trips had been made to Bevilport before

[24] Andrew F. Smyth account books, 1865–1868. AFS MSS.
[25] Andrew F. Smyth field notes for the 1860's. AFS MSS.

the war, but some of the boats had fallen apart or had been destroyed during the wartime business slump. The boats, therefore, were not seen as frequently at Bevilport as they had been. The need for a steamer which would travel from Sabine Pass to Bevilport and back again was evident. Such a boat would have no trouble attracting customers. In fact, could not a store and steamboat work hand in hand? Andrew pondered the matter.

IV

Andrew took a flatboat to Sabine Pass in early fall, 1869. Perhaps needing some goods not available at the Pass, he went to Galveston. In Galveston he was told of an old steamer named the *Camargo* which was being sold by her owners.[26] The asking price was about $4,000; of course, this was too much, for the boat was dilapidated, but even at that price he felt that she could probably pay for herself in a few years on the rivers —an opinion which showed less concern for glamour in a boat than usefulness. Andrew arranged to have his purchases forwarded upriver and headed for home.

Back in Bevilport he approached Elias Seale with the idea of forming a company which would buy the steamboat. Owning a store himself, Elias was aware of the need for fast, regular transportation from the coast to the backwoods. Besides stocking Bevilport stores, the steamboat owners could fill individual orders just as Andrew had been doing for years on the keelboats; and a steamer could carry more than twice as many cotton bales as the *Jasper* had. Characteristically, Elias thrust himself into the project, certain that this would become the nucleus of great riches to come. Reaching an agreement with a Mr. Hadnot, a local businessman and farmer, Andrew and Elias planned to buy a boat. Each investor would own a third. The three, having gone to Galveston to see the *Camargo*, decided to try to find a better boat for the $3,000 which they had said they would spend. Since Andrew would be captain of the new boat, he was sent to New Orleans, Cincinnati, and Evansville, Indiana, to see what he could find. Leaving October 4 he made the long journey and took notes of what he saw. It was Andrew's first visit to the North; maybe he wondered how runaway Jim had fared in this country, which was supposed to be so different from home. He was back in Bevilport in a month and a half, empty handed. He just couldn't find any

---

[26] [?], Galveston, Texas, to V. Wiess, September [?]. A note telling of the steamer *Camargo*. AFS MSS.

$3,000 steamboats or at least none that the three partners would consider investing in. Many fine boats were for sale, to be sure, but their prices far exceeded what Smyth, Seale, and Hadnot wanted to pay. Steamboats were very much in demand.

In Galveston the three bargained with the owners of the *Camargo*. The price was finally lowered to $3,000 and on December 17 the papers were signed.[27] The *Camargo* was a stubby, square-nosed boat with one cramped cabin, a pilot house, a stern wheel, and a vast, open deck. She could carry three hundred bales of cotton and when the cotton was unloaded ample space was available for barrels and cases of goods.[28] An advertisement for cargo was placed in the Jasper newspaper.

As Andrew's term as chief justice of the county ended during the summer of 1869, he could assume the duties of captain in January, 1870, the time when the *Camargo* was brought upriver. He had decided a year before not to run again for judge and he had spent his free time during the fall searching for a boat. Farmers who did not have river landings of their own, or whose landings were too far up the Angelina to be wholly accessible, hauled their cotton to Bevilport, where the *Camargo* was tied up. As in the days of keelboats and flatboats, the cotton was checked to see that it was properly marked with the owners' initials.

Taking orders for flour, coffee, hoop skirts, plows, nails, and the like, the boat moved from the dock downriver toward Sabine Pass. The usual stops were made along the river: Town Bluff, Wiess's Bluff, Bunn's Bluff, Beaumont, and the many private landings. When the *Camargo* first began the Bevilport to Sabine Pass trips orders for merchandise included only occasional items which were not necessities. People were still building their farms back to what they had been before the war. No money could be spared for luxuries.

The *Camargo* owners did not take long to realize that she was not much easier to handle than a keelboat. Her only real advantage over the earlier vessel was her tolerable steam engine. At times low water made it impossible for the boat to leave the Bevilport landing, but this condition was true of any form of river travel even though most of the trip was made on improved waters. When the steamer was in the current, however, she was nearly impossible to manage; a moment's neglect of the wheel could send her lumbering uncontrollably toward the river-

[27] "Steamer Camargo and owners in Account with Hobby and Post," Galveston, Texas, January 15, 1870. AFS MSS.
[28] *The Beaumont Journal,* Beaumont, Texas, September 12, 1925, Sec. 2, p. 1 (clipping).

bank and possible disaster. On many occasions she got out of hand, jerked and swerved, and sent cotton bales toppling into the water, in which case all hands on board jumped for grappling hooks so that the cotton could be recovered before it became saturated and sank.

Although passengers were happy to have so ready a means of riding upriver, they complained of the inconvenient cabin, where ladies, having no other place to sit, were exposed to spittoons, whiskey, and men's loud talking. The boat, however, was a money-maker for the company. Andrew and his fellow steamboat owners battled with their *Camargo*, finally paying for her in the summer of 1871.[29]

When the $3,000 debt on the boat was paid, the company could take home greater profits. Very little had evidently been spent on the upkeep of the *Camargo* since it had been bought by the Bevilport men. The steamer became a constant worry to her owners, for they never knew when she would take that final plunge into the riverbank.

By autumn, 1871, Andrew had become weary of this boat. On a certain trip downriver that season, the steamer got furiously out of hand, her steering mechanism completely broken beyond use. The boat went fast with the current, speeding from one side of the river to the other, bumping into fallen logs hanging from the riverbank, then zig-zagging toward the opposite shore. It was fortunate that she missed the underwater snags. Finally she lunged into a marshy area and was stopped by the tough cypress trees. She reposed there, steam boiling from her stack. Andrew, in one of his temper flares, declared, "Never again!"[30]

[29] Hobby and Post, Galveston, Texas, to Andrew F. Smyth, August 10, 1871. A copy. AFS MSS.

[30] *The Beaumont Journal,* Beaumont, Texas, September 12, 1925, Sec. 2, p. 1 (clipping).

11. When the cantankerous *Camargo* was back at the Bevilport landing Andrew met with Elias and Mr. Hadnot. He advised them that the steamer had become almost more trouble than it was worth. Since good money was to be made from river transportation, why not buy a better boat? It was agreed that the *Camargo* should be sold. Andrew and Elias were in favor of buying another boat. But Mr. Hadnot, while he did not object to the disposal of the *Camargo*, did not want to enter another such river business. It was settled that the *Camargo* was up for sale. The problem remained to find men willing to invest in a new boat.

I

Andrew liked the idea of remaining a steamer captain and he sent letters to the various people that he thought might be interested in buying into a new boat. On the river again regularly after several years of only occasional flatboat trips, he was determined to stay. The *Camargo* had served its purpose but now Andrew wanted something better, a steamer which would give him the same prestige on the river that he enjoyed on land.

Colonel C. R. Beaty, a prominent resident of Jasper, approached Andrew and Elias, saying that he would definitely like to participate if another company formed. Beaty contacted his friend, Colonel P. F. Renfro, who lived in Sabine Pass but was giving serious consideration to re-establishing himself in Jasper County. Renfro was a successful merchant and he, as much as any of the other three, realized the virtues of a steamboat company. The new boat, they all agreed, must be big enough to carry large quantities of cotton and merchandise, as well as have comfortable quarters for passengers.

Andrew and Elias would each invest $3,250, while the colonels, somewhat more conservative, supplied $1,500, jointly. The investors wanted another $1,000. James Lee, a merchant, and James Bean, a preacher, both of Magnolia Springs, entered the company with $500 each. Having $9,000 to deal with, the company counted itself able to buy what it wanted. Smyth, they said, would be captain of the new boat.[1]

---

[1] Andrew F. Smyth account book, 1871; *The Sunday Enterprise,* Beaumont, Texas, November 27, 1932, p. 8–A (clipping).

Because Andrew, Elias, and the colonels did not have sufficient ready cash to supply the amounts which they had agreed to invest, they went to Galveston to Hobby and Post, a large mercantile house. Coastal firms of this kind were often quite willing to finance backwoods shipping enterprises, for improved transportation on the rivers was an asset to their business. Hobby and Post had lent a small sum toward the purchase of the *Camargo* and they were happy to underwrite $8,000 on the new steamboat.[2]

Examining boats for sale at the Galveston dock, none of the investors seemed pleased. It was decided that Andrew, being captain, would leave at once for New Orleans, and if no likely steamers were there he would visit the shipyards of the upper Mississippi and, if necessary, the Ohio as well. Elias and Mr. Hadnot, meanwhile, would sell the *Camargo*.

Andrew left Bevilport on October 8, 1871, carrying a letter of credit from Hobby and Post, his baggage, and an old army pistol, which was issued to him during the war. From Galveston he went to New Orleans.

There were probably a number of steamboats for sale at New Orleans but none of them appealed to him, for he headed up the Mississippi soon after he arrived in the city. After traveling for three weeks aboard a steamer he was in Cincinnati; he had not stopped along the way. Even the Cincinnati shipyards offered nothing. Evidently, by this time Andrew had decided exactly what he wanted; and since he would be captain of this new boat, it would meet the requirements if he had to build it himself. By November 1 he had retraced his steps as far as Evansville, Indiana.[3]

Beside the Evansville wharf was a steamer for sale, which was, to the inch, what Andrew had been looking for. The price of the steamer was far more than $9,000. Andrew talked with the owners and they reluctantly lowered their price to $11,000, saying that they would positively take no less. That price was, of course, out of the question, almost as much as the original one had been. Four days of examining other boats accomplished nothing, for no other river packet could compare with the one he had seen first. They were either too big or too small, too fancy or too plain.

Andrew thought of the $11,000 as he surveyed the pleasing lines of the steamboat. She was 115 feet long and had a 32-foot beam. Her two levels of decks were well made, glowing under a coat of white paint. On

[2] Hobby and Post receipt, presumably at Galveston, Texas, September 12, 1871. AFS MSS.
[3] Expense account for the trip to Ohio, October 8, 1871. AFS MSS.

the upper deck were lines of green doors, which led to the passenger cabins and the saloon. She was a stern-wheeler and on each side in big letters was painted her name, *Laura*. The cabins were typically tiny but built with a close attention to detail. Five were on each side of the boat. Down the center of the second level extended the saloon.

In that room were arm chairs, sofas, a big mahogany sideboard, pictures and mirrors, a square grand piano, and a long table with chairs pulled up to it. A tall iron stove served to heat the room, and the many doors onto the decks had louvered inserts, which could be opened to catch breezes in the summer. The walls of the saloon were white with green trim like everything else on the boat.

An uncovered staircase led from the second deck to the first level, where there was a huge storage area for freight. She was, in fact, primarily a freight boat. On the roof, overlooking the whole boat, was the pilothouse. On it, too, was painted the name *Laura*.[4] The forty-horsepower engine was modern and in good condition, certainly an improvement over that of the *Camargo*. Thinking as he looked, Andrew realized that the *Laura* was too good to pass up.[5]

The *Laura* was a boat that a man could be proud of. For years Andrew had floated into Sabine Lake in gawky flatboats. Then he had built the *Jasper*, which at that time was an admirable vessel. With the *Jasper* he had learned what it was like to be the master of a good boat. It was a feeling that neither the sawmill nor the prospect of a store could ever replace in him. The awkward old *Camargo* was an unsightly thing that a captain rather preferred to slip into port than to land dramatically.

While Andrew had made many friends on the river and was respected, he wanted a boat that people might envy and praise, a boat which would add prestige to the name of the captain. The *Laura* was just such a boat.

To buy the steamer *Laura* would mean taking the risk of infuriating the other investors. They were interested only in the revenue which the business would bring. For Andrew it was a different matter. Money was important to be sure, but he and Emily had all they wanted at home. Here was the chance to have something more than money. It was the opportunity to command splendor itself—a fresh, white steamer to be shown off like a toy at the river settlements and rushed to the wharves at the Pass in a dark cloud of smoke with screaming whistles. The time had

[4] Mrs. George C. O'Brien to author in a conversation, July 10, 1962.

[5] *The Beaumont Journal,* Beaumont, Texas, September 12, 1925, Sec. 2, p. 1 (clipping).

come to emerge from the sweat of the mill, the loneliness of the flatboat and the transit, and become the captain of the finest, most luxurious means of transportation that the Neches River had ever seen. On his last buying trip many thousands had stood between him and a good steamboat, but now things were different.

Arrangements were made by mail with Hobby and Post for the extra $2,000.[6] When the Galveston firm replied that they would finance "anything Judge Smyth elects to purchase," the sale was made.[7] Andrew's partners in Sabine Pass, Bevilport, Magnolia Springs, and Jasper, unaware of their newest debt, would hear the whole story in due time. At the moment, the partners were far from Andrew Smyth's thoughts.

The trip home would be made down the Ohio and the Mississippi. Supplies had to be bought, because the *Laura* had lain idle for many months. Food, fuel, and, not least, deck stoves, for the river air would be very cold, were acquired at Evansville supply houses. Talking to the eleven men, one by one, Andrew hired the entire crew that had been with the steamer before. Their salaries were decided on the spot, but payment was undoubtedly promised at a later date. The names were meticulously listed in the account book:[8]

Harry Gains—Mate.   Began work Monday Nov. 13 at $40/month.
McGennis—Watchman.   Started 16 Nov. at $25/month.
John Houston—Engineer.   Started Nov. 16 at $100/Month.
John Zipler—Deck Hand.   Started Nov. 16 at $25/Month.
Allen N. Short—Started Nov. 16 at $25/month.
Scott, Billings, John & a fireman—All started Nov. 16 at $25/month.
James—Cook.   started Nov. 16 at $25/month.
John Piles—Engineer.   Started Nov. 23 at $3/day.

As the list of supplies could not be filled entirely in Evansville the *Laura* was taken up to Cincinnati. Interested in making money from the voyage to Texas, Andrew advertised in a Cincinnati newspaper for Sabine Pass- or Galveston-bound freight. A furniture manufacturer contacted him and the boat was loaded with household goods.[9] About November 20 Andrew and his crew of eleven headed down the Ohio toward Cairo, Illinois, where they entered the Mississippi.

Once on the Mississippi, the *Laura* must indeed have looked small and

[6] Hobby and Post, Galveston, Texas, to Andrew F. Smyth, November 5, 1871. AFS MSS.

[7] *Ibid.*

[8] Expense account for the trip to Ohio, October 8, 1871. AFS MSS.

[9] *Ibid.*

felt even smaller when she rocked over waves created by the great river packets. Andrew was learning more about steamboating than he had learned in his whole career as captain of the *Camargo*.

After what probably seemed like a long time the *Laura* passed New Orleans and was in the Gulf of Mexico. Because the steamer was no match for the turbid waters of the Gulf, she was kept as close to the shore as possible. At night she was guided into some bayou or cove, there to remain until morning. The daytime trip was hard enough but to have tried to navigate at night would have been foolish.

Shortly after Christmas the *Laura* was at the Sabine Pass wharf, where her cargo was unloaded, some of it to be shipped on to Galveston aboard another vessel.[10] It was good that people at the Pass looked approvingly at Andrew's steamer. There had been times when he had entered the pass more humbly; actually, this introduction of the *Laura* into Texas gave Andrew a proud feeling which he had not experienced since the days of the *Jasper*. The *Jasper* was now a memory, its parts woven into the fabric of the house back home. But Andrew had not forgotten the grand feeling of being master of an admirable boat.

He stopped at the landings on the way to Bevilport, eager to impress those who remembered the *Camargo* on the Neches; the *Laura* looked big and fine. Her whistle was loud and she made waves that splashed against the riverbanks on both sides. If she had been a little sheepish on the Mississippi, here was her glory; for she met no equal in bigness, whiteness, or just plain stylishness.[11] How proud Andrew must have been—how delighted Emily would be.

The partners would object to the purchase price but they could not help but like their beautiful *Laura*. It was odd that Andrew, for once, had thought so little of his partners in the homeward trip.

When finally the *Laura* docked at Bevilport, local people swarmed to see her. Farmers and townspeople pushed in, examining the snug staterooms with their built-in bunks and the almost elegant decorations of the saloon. Andrew patiently pointed out this or that fine feature, telling at the same time how adventurous the trip down the Ohio, the Mississippi, and into the Gulf had been.

Since it took time to get the word around, the tour lasted several days. Meanwhile, Andrew met with Elias, the colonels, James Lee, and James Bean. They were very happy with the new boat until they discovered

---

[10] *The Beaumont Journal*, Beaumont, Texas, September 12, 1925, Sec. 2, p. 1 (clipping).
[11] Mrs. George C. O'Brien to author in a conversation, July 10, 1962.

how much she had cost. Expressions altered. Had they not told Andrew exactly what they could afford to spend? How could he assume the responsibility of putting the company deeper in debt? Andrew's partners were disgusted, but they, like Andrew, did not want to part with *Laura*.[12] The threat to sell the boat was the captain's ammunition against their attacks and he won. If the venture resulted in failure, they reminded Andrew, it would be his fault. An advertisement was placed in *The Jasper Newsboy*, the newspaper lately established by a former New Orleans newsboy to replace the old paper which had closed during the war.

The *Laura's* first official voyage from Bevilport commenced in January, 1872. Cotton was shipped to Sabine Pass at two dollars per bale. As before, the captain was to arrange for its storage at the Pass and its delivery to Galveston or New Orleans. The *Laura* could carry six hundred bales at one time. Almost no limit was placed on the amount of merchandise which people could order from the coast for shipment aboard the *Laura*. She could carry 1,700 barrels and several hundred boxes and cases besides, when the cotton was unloaded.[13] Comfortable cabin accommodations could be had for fifteen dollars and the trip to Sabine Pass took from eighteen to twenty-two days. Meals were prepared on board by James, a Negro cook who came from Evansville, and Nero, a Negro who had been with the *Camargo*. Both men gained reputations as excellent cooks.

Nine Negroes were employed for work on the *Laura*, and, besides Andrew, four white men, including Sam Morris and Harry Gains. In the coming years the Evansville men would return to Indiana, leaving the *Laura* with a crew of local men. On the first trip from Bevilport to Sabine Pass the steamer was loaded with several hundred bales of cotton and her cabins were all occupied. All the members of the crew were aboard.

The partners decided to share equally in the extra $2,000 that Andrew had spent. Andrew was placed on a salary, which was a commission above his regular share of the profits of each voyage. His debt was $3,450. Applying to this amount his return from the sale of the *Camargo*, he reduced his debt to $1,900. He paid this to Hobby and Post in installments.[14]

[12] *The Beaumont Journal,* Beaumont, Texas, September 12, 1925, Sec. 2, p. 1 (clipping).
[13] *The Sunday Enterprise,* Beaumont, Texas, November 27, 1932, p. 8–A (clipping).
[14] Hobby and Post, Galveston, Texas, to Andrew F. Smyth, March [?], 1872. AFS MSS.

A downriver trip on the *Laura* differed little from the same trip on a keelboat except that steamboat travel was easier and more comfortable. Either Andrew or the mate stayed in the high pilothouse at the wheel at all times. While the boat was moving, the deckhands had little to do, but when a landing was reached they were expected to work hard unloading and loading freight. At Sabine Pass their duties were increased, for the entire cargo had to be unloaded and taken to a warehouse.

Andrew's daughter, Minty, recalled the activity at the wharves:[15]

It was a great sight when the whistle would blow for some of the landings to see all the people hurrying to the riverbank. I can see now the Negroes carrying sides of bacon and other goods on their heads from the deck of the Laura to the shore and just as if it were yesterday I can hear them singing their favorite song: "I'm all the way from Phil-a-del-fee-ah!" There was always a lot of singing among the Negro deckhands as they unloaded and loaded freight.

James and Nero were busy most of the time cooking meals on the wood-burning kitchen stove, dusting and sweeping in the passengers' quarters, or pouring drinks at the bar. It was not really a hard life. Once the men had become used to the routine of steamboat operation, they knew that there was a moment to act and work hard and that there was a time for unworried relaxation. The man at the wheel had to keep alert watching for turns and dangerous spots in the river. After several trips he grew accustomed to the path of the rivers and although new obstructions appeared each time, he too could assume a relaxed air.

Passengers lounged on the deck, in their cramped cabins, or in the saloon. Within the saloon was a well-stocked bar, where men could procure tumblers of whiskey and ladies could enjoy elderberry wine or brandied cherries. More often, however, the saloon was a place where passengers relaxed, sitting to smoke, read, or talk.[16] For short trips people seldom occupied a cabin, preferring to sit in the saloon until their destination was reached. The most inexpensive ticket was "deck passage" which entitled the buyer to a place on the lower deck without the benefit of a cabin, the saloon, or meals. Such a ticket cost between six and eight dollars for the twenty-two–day Sabine Pass to Bevilport run.[17] Traveling in the saloon meant wearing one's Sunday best, enjoying the atmosphere of a party.

[15] *The Beaumont Journal,* Beaumont, Texas, September 12, 1925, Sec. 2, p. 1 (clipping).
[16] Mrs. George C. O'Brien to author in a conversation, July 10, 1962.
[17] Andrew F. Smyth account book, 1873. AFS MSS.

When the *Laura* stopped at a river town, farmers, merchants, and townspeople went to the wharves either to transact business or simply to see what freight and passengers were aboard. From riverbottom cotton fields Negroes ran to the fence and waved at the steamer, knowing that they would be answered by a loud blast of the whistle. Now and then a little party of travelers stood with their baggage at the river's edge, far from town, and waved handkerchiefs, signifying that they wanted to come aboard; the flat-bottomed steamer then sided to the riverbank, lowered the gangplank, and admitted the new passengers.

Some days were placid, when the river was rather still and the *Laura* slid ahead full steam, looking clean and white against the brown water and the lush green of the woods on either side. At other times rain fell so solidly that the river could hardly be seen before the boat. Even on hot, sunny days black clouds might appear in the north. When that happened, everyone on board knew that the cold winds and rains of a Texas norther were not far away.

From the pilothouse Andrew saw things, removed, his thoughts rambling. On the wharves or the decks he felt conspicuous. And he liked to feel that way.

II

The *Laura* was extremely profitable for her owners. Late in 1875 Hobby and Post had their $10,000 in hand, paid in full.[18] The delighted owners forgave Andrew for spending more than he should have. In that year, 1875, his salary was raised 2 per cent, making his intake from each trip 10 per cent of the profit, besides his regular share in the company. From now on Andrew would have no money problems.

During January, 1876, Andrew unlocked his Bevilport store and opened for business. His stock included linens, brocade, towel cloth, and cotton cloth; tooth brushes, powders, cure-alls, and "liver regulation prepared and unprepared"; curry combs, shovels, axes, rifles, and "iron spoons" both for "table and tea"; dresses, silk vests, broadcloth suits, palmetto hats, men's brogans, and "ladies fancy slippers"; stationery, gold pens, spelling books, knitting needles, and "stone and wood pipes" —in short, anything anybody could possibly need.[19] Whiskey, one of the most common commodities in country stores, was not handled by An-

[18] Hobby and Post, Galveston, Texas, to Andrew F. Smyth, November 17, 1875. AFS MSS.

[19] Orders from Sabine Pass and Galveston for the "Bevilport Store," January 1, 1876. AFS MSS.

drew, probably because of the temperance movement, which was fast taking hold in the county.

Elias had closed his store at the end of 1875 and Andrew, eager to establish an additional source of income, wanted to supply the replacement. This new store began on a better footing than had the one in the fifties. The sawmill still operated but it was no longer significant in Andrew's business life. Placing a manager in charge of the store, Andrew handled the bookkeeping himself and remained in his position as captain of the *Laura*. Although not as large as some of the other stores in Bevilport, Smyth's General Merchandise was a success almost as soon as its doors opened.[20] In time, the captain said, George and Buddy would be out of school and could run the store.

While there were people who had not done well in Texas in the years since the Civil War, Andrew could certainly not complain. In Jasper County he owned some 3,000 acres besides several town lots in Bevilport; he had 1,476 acres in Tyler County, sixteen town lots at Sabine Pass, and fourteen sections—8,960 acres—in West Texas, which had been taken in part payment for his services as subengineer in the river project.[21] An inventory of his land was impressive to one who was unaware that land and income were sometimes unrelated. Andrew's money came from the *Laura* and the store in Bevilport, a small return came from them and the mill, but the solid profit he had once made from lumber was a thing of the past. With the exception of the home place all his land was being held until someone offered a good price for it.

When the *Laura* docked at Sabine Pass, Andrew usually went to Galveston, traveling along the beach where the broken hulls of ships were the only obstructions to the fast stagecoach. Galveston was a tropical place of orange, oak, and palm trees, its streets lined with tall shuttered houses raised high off the ground. The contrast of the beautiful and the ugly was there. Prosperous business houses with iron-work decorations faced low-class shops and saloons of wood. The residences of the rich merchants loomed behind white painted fences, which enclosed shady gardens; but the poor sections of the city had shoddy, unpainted hovels, exposed to the hot sun. And nowhere was the sun hotter at certain times of the year. In striking contrast to the cheap hotels of the waterfront was

[20] Evidence in Andrew F. Smyth's account books for 1876 through 1879. AFS MSS.

[21] Receipt for land-tax payment, 1875. AFS MSS.

the sumptuous Tremont House, famous for its hospitality and elegance. On more than one occasion Andrew patronized the dining room and bar of this hotel, though he was hardly the type to pay a premium to sit amidst elegance.

Besides enjoying the many obvious attractions of the city, Andrew liked to breathe the salt breeze and bathe in the waves of the Gulf of Mexico, undisturbed, relaxed. It was pleasant to walk on the beach after a busy day in the offices of Hobby and Post or Ball, Hutchings, and Company. For years he made a practice of staying at the quiet Washington Hotel, first called the Ohio House, a great frame structure with comfortable, inexpensive accommodations and a good dining room.

After a time, in Galveston, the salt breeze began to feel dirty and the noise of so many people made Andrew long for the quiet of home. He was glad that these business trips were short, for he tired of crowded places.

Leaving Galveston, he returned to Sabine Pass to see that the *Laura* was loaded, and headed upriver. Again at Bevilport the farmers were given their cotton or produce money, and people flocked to the gangplank to meet passengers or to have their goods transferred to waiting wagons. At the table in the *Laura's* saloon, the six owners divided their earnings from the trip, giving Andrew his share of the profits and deducting from each man's percentage the expenses which the boat had incurred.[22]

To all who knew the rivers Andrew had become Captain Smyth. It was a title not new in his family, though never before had it seemed so significant. Once he had been called "Squire Smyth," and more recently "Judge Smyth." Neither title meant much to him. It was Captain that he liked to be, and at last he was that, from Galveston to Bevilport. The *Laura* became a dependable means of transportation for people all along the river, and Captain Smyth grew in importance. A veteran riverman recalled in later years, "It was unthinkable to have anybody but Captain Smyth in command of the *Laura*; a change would almost have brought on a revolution up river."[23] The smallest farm or village was familiar with the *Laura* and her Captain.

Andrew was recognized even on the streets of the larger places like

[22] Andrew Smyth's account books for the 1870's. AFS MSS.
[23] *The Beaumont Journal,* Beaumont, Texas, September 12, 1925, Sec. 2, p. 1 (clipping).

Beaumont and Sabine Pass. Now and then he was greeted pleasantly on Galveston sidewalks by someone who knew him. Not to be forgotten was the good name that he had built and kept in his own Jasper County. A good name had always meant much to Andrew F. Smyth. Had he taken the time to consider the matter he might well have congratulated himself on the successful results of his labors.

12. Because Andrew was away from home a great part of the time Emily, when her domestic duties were not pressing, occasionally made trips downriver with him. With few exceptions though, Andrew left his family behind. Frances Grigsby Smyth maintained her farm as always, needing Mammy Silla as Mammy Silla needed her. George, Jr., handled her business affairs and saw that she had money to keep her home as it was and to make a yearly trip to Austin to visit George's grave. Her youngest child had already finished school. Emily frequently called on Frances at Walnut Run and Frances traveled to Emily's house quite as often.[1]

I

Of Andrew and Emily's children, Minty, George, and Buddy remained at home. Susan, now Mrs. Hart, was living in Jasper; Frances, Mrs. Shelby, lived near Indian Creek on a farm that Andrew had given her as a wedding present. Elisha and Nancy and their many children had moved to Hopewell, a neighborhood in Tyler County, only a half-day's ride from Bevilport. Emily felt that she now could travel with her husband from time to time aboard the *Laura*. She had seen very little of cities in her life and the reaction of his country wife to fast-moving places amused Andrew greatly.

On a trip to Galveston in about 1875 Andrew and Emily had a tintype made of themselves together. Andrew at fifty-eight was showing signs of age. His hair was streaked with gray at the temples, and his face lacked the fullness that it had once had. Yet in this tintype he smirked as merrily as he had in the daguerreotype taken in New Orleans thirty years before. Had his prosperous slouch not given him away, one might have thought him little different from the poor but ambitious young man who had traveled far to meet the Kentucky girl. Emily, now forty-eight, sat beside him smiling as much as her dignity would allow. Her hair too was gray-streaked, but her carriage had changed very little; she was still as erect and neat as she had always been. Time had given a certain grace to the wife of Andrew Smyth. Very much had happened in these years.

---

[1] Emily Allen Smyth, Bevilport, Texas, to "sister," February 28, 1882. AFS MSS.

Andrew and Emily's way of life had not been altered by the success of the *Laura* and the store. Perhaps they had planned to build a new house on their lots in Bevilport. But when the time came to build, had not the old house seemed good enough, after all?

Even if the rooms were still unfinished and their wooden walls had turned dark, worn to the point of looking homey, they were cluttered with beloved mementos like seashells from the Gulf and family pictures and the odds and ends of many years of hard use. New chairs and tables had been acquired and mixed in with the old. On a trip to Galveston, Andrew had bought a square grand piano and presented it to Minty on her sixteenth birthday.[2] It stood in the front room designated as the "boys' room." Andrew's safe and desk were there as well, for when it was needed the boys' room was a farm and mill office. Andrew also had an office aboard the *Laura* and one on the second floor of the Bevilport store. Directly across the entry from the boys' room was Andrew and Emily's room, which served as a parlor, as well. Behind the two front rooms and the entry were a bedroom, a pantry, a partially enclosed porch, a weaving and spinning room leading to the rear breezeway, and, beyond, the dining room and kitchen, neither of which had glass windows, only batten shutters.

A number of Negro families had been hired to work on the place. Their houses were scattered along the road before the main house and on the road to the mill. After the war Ann had taken her two sons and had gone North, or so she claimed. She had returned once, but because she was impudent and refused to work once too often, she had been ordered to leave. A new Ann had taken her place. As this woman was married to a man named Tobe, she was called Ann-Tobe to distinguish her from the other Ann. Ann-Tobe was always within calling distance, for the cook's house, where she lived, adjoined the backyard. A pleasant woman, dedicated to Emily, she rose to a position of great responsibility on the farm.

At the edge of the pear orchard across from the main house, a blacksmith shop had been built, which served the needs of the *Laura* and the farm. Tobe could work there during his time off and accept pay from customers in the neighborhood. The Smyth farm was, as before, busy and noisy on every day except Sunday, when few people were there. Little children were underfoot—now usually the children of the Negroes, unless the Smyths' grandchildren happened to be visiting "Mommey" and "Grandpa," as they sometimes were from May to August.

[2] Mrs. Kern Braswell, Andrew's granddaughter, to author in a conversation, July 19, 1962.

Andrew and Emily enjoyed their farm to the fullest. In the midst of continual work they truly believed that this particular property was always beautiful. Summer meant hot sun but an abundance of good things to eat; autumn was a time of muted colors in the woods, and the rain which soon filled the swamp, sending creatures crawling to dry land; the winter was cool enough most of the time to drive the family close to the fireside; and spring was the time of dogwood, of garden blooms, flowers from the seed catalog, and of refreshing river breezes. It was beautiful because it was home, the place to which they were tied from the depths of themselves.

In this certain week of the year, mattresses and quilts were hung on the fence to sun—in that month no one would consider missing cane grinding. At sundown Andrew and Emily loved to walk in the woods; those same woods which once had been a towering obstacle to strip from the earth, they now allowed to grow over most of the land, and to the shadowed forest they attributed a magical quality, an aura of wonder, of delight.[3]

The farm itself was not profitable, but it was not intended to be so.[4] Still, the fields produced vegetables, fruit, and some cotton; in the woods were deer, squirrels, and wild fowl, not to mention the various domestic animals kept in the pastures. From it all came an abundant table. This was what the Smyths asked of the land.

Had it not been for this land, the home that he loved and had almost lost, Andrew could never have sensed the full enjoyment of being Captain Smyth. For it was this place years ago that had taught him how blind men often are to the good of the moment, seeing only some distant greatness which they label happiness.[5]

Sabine Pass now had six thousand inhabitants, most of whom made a living in one way or another from this gateway to the Gulf. Beaumont, having flowered as a sawmill center, rambled its unpainted way along the Neches River with many new citizens. In fact, the lumber industry caused the growth of these downriver towns and the decline of those upriver. Timber cut from the woods was thrown into the Neches and thousands of logs at a time were floated downriver to the mills along the way to the Gulf. This practice was now a worse impediment to river travel than it ever had been.

[3] Andrew F. Smyth, Bevilport, Texas, to M. C. Smyth, July [?], 1878. AFS MSS.

[4] Account books and farm notes, 1850–1859; 1876–1885. AFS MSS.

[5] Mrs. George C. O'Brien in a conversation with the author, July 10, 1962.

Although Bevilport looked much as it had for the past twenty years, the observant noticed changes. Several stores, including Elias Seale's, stood boarded up. The hotel did not register nearly as many guests as it once had. The boom in building ended early in these years of the seventies.

The *Laura* kept her place, for the river was yet the quickest route from the backwoods to the coast and the towns in-between. She was the first dependable steamboat that the Neches had known. But the *Laura* was having to alter her schedule at times to avoid the floating logs, and her owners must have sensed that someday the railroad would grow enough to end her career. Fortunately the coming of the railroad seemed a long way off. For the time the *Laura* did well. She was kept clean and painted, and seldom was she not loaded with cotton, produce, dry goods, and passengers.

Jasper still thrived. New houses were built, old ones torn down. The town was rather as it had been except for a few conspicuous places where a cottage had given way to a fussy house of gingerbread and stained glass. The South East Texas Male and Female College opened in the autumn of 1878 with an enrollment of ninety-two; local students were having the advantage of good teachers and fine facilities. Proud of their college, Jasper people spoke of their town as "The Athens of Texas," a title claimed by many Texas towns. Buddy, who had attended school in Texarkana, came home to enter classes at the new college at Jasper, probably at Andrew and Emily's insistence.

The 1870's were years when things seemed on the verge of a great change. Coastal cities rose, and conveniences like railroads were coming into common use. The people of the smallest towns in Jasper County, as everywhere in Texas, believed that their town would someday rival Galveston or the growing Houston. Time, they said, would prove them right.

Andrew and Emily enjoyed the social life of the county. The prominent names in the county were not different from what they had been before the war: Ryall, Neyland, Adams, Kelly, Ford, Lanier, McFarland, White, Stone, Norsworthy, Trotty, and so on. They were still the big farmers and the big merchants.

The social sphere in which the Smyths moved was the same, but people had become more imaginative in their entertainments. Such elegant games as croquet were played, along with countless parlor games, popular even with people who did not have parlors and most in fact did not yet have such luxuries. Young people organized botany clubs in an effort to free themselves from the puritanical stares of their elders.[6] More or less in line with the clubs' supposed purposes young men aimed rifles and shot mistletoe or magnolia blooms from the trees to present to the young ladies. Other than that it is recalled that little botany was absorbed.

One day each year was set aside for the Tournament. No stores stayed open during this event, as the populace prepared for a picnic. The highlight of the day was the actual tournament, which a Jasper lady commented was "exactly like Sir Walter Scott's stories."[7] A section of the Bevilport Road, just outside the town, was reserved, an archway was made from blossoms and greenery, and a number of rings were suspended from ribbons in the openings. When the signal was given, as many riders as there were rings rushed on decorated mounts from a concealed place toward the archway. They were disguised in knightly robes of silk or satin and held long spears thrust forward. Spurring his mount to a fast gallop, each of the riders aimed his spear at a certain ring. An instant later they pulled to a halt. When the dust had cleared, the judges stepped close to see which riders had captured rings. The winners were honored at the picnic and dance which followed.[8] And incidentally they selected the girl who would be queen of the ball and were her escorts for the evening.

On the appropriate anniversaries each year veterans of the Texas Revolution, the Mexican War, and the Civil War had a parade followed by speeches. Captain Kellie's Jefferson Rifles, named for Jefferson Davis, marched on the Bevilport Road and around the courthouse square. By the 1870's the members of the Jasper Volunteers of 1836 were honored by Captain Kellie with carriages so that they would not have to walk in the parades. These days were patriotic holidays dedicated more to the old than the young.

But any day was unusual when one could not find a group of war veterans sitting on the courthouse square, chewing tobacco and talking. Some of these men had been prominent farmers when Andrew first came to the region. Now their sons tried to squeeze a living from the soil or held jobs elsewhere, making it possible for the old men to retire.

[6] Mrs. Charles Martin to the author in conversation, August 5, 1962.

[7] Mrs. George C. O'Brien in a conversation with the author, July 10, 1962.

[8] Mrs. George C. O'Brien in conversation with the author; Andrew F. Smyth account book, 1852. AFS MSS.

The old men of the courthouse square played cards and talked quietly most of the time, but on days when the town was crowded certain ones of them took great pleasure in harassing people.

Old age, more than good taste, gave the speakers privileges which younger men did not share. Elisha Seale recalled that once while Emily shopped, Andrew joined a merry group which had gathered to encourage a frisky visitor from Tyler County, who had come to call on an old friend, a former judge whom he had fought beside in the Revolution. For a change of subject matter, Andrew mischievously asked the bearded speaker, who was not more than twelve years his senior, what he thought of heredity. At about that time one of two brothers who owned a store shouted across the street, demanding that the old man keep his conversation down because he was embarrassing lady customers in the store. Both of the storeowners then stood in the street to see if the ultimatum would be heeded. Indignantly, the old man stood tall on a stepping block and addressed himself to Andrew in somewhat the following manner:

Sir, you have solicited my opinion on the subject of heredity. I will answer right off that I believe in heredity. For a long time I thought it was foolish. But I know for a fact that the father of those two storekeepers over there went to the Mexican War and suffered from diarrhea from the opening of the war to the end. Today his sons are the biggest two turds in Jasper County. I ask you, sir, is that not evidence of heredity?

Andrew's reply, if he made one, is not remembered.

Not all the old men on the square were retired from business; it was simply the gathering place of their contemporaries, the spot where they could talk over old times in the manner they liked best; therefore, they went to the square. Andrew might well have wondered what George's opinion of life on the courthouse square would have been had he lived. George W. Smyth would probably have stayed in his library, anyway, until he could no longer see the print on the page. Then perhaps he would have gone to town.

Still only two churches were represented in the county, the Methodist and the Baptist. The Baptist was predominant, having congregations throughout the countryside. In Jasper, Methodist and Baptist services were held on alternate Sundays. Essentially the congregations were the same, for on Baptist Sundays the Methodists appeared in full force, and, likewise, the Baptists went to Methodist services. While Dixie Church served the Negroes in the Indian Creek neighborhood, Jasper Negroes attended church with the white people, using the gallery just as they had before the war. Churches often held barbecues and fun-raising carnivals that complemented the private parties, which helped keep the people socially occupied.

Andrew and Emily liked such functions and occasionally invited people to their own house for a dance or barbecue. At such times, horse races, a shooting match or two, or perhaps a hunt in the swamp filled the afternoon. The favorite sport of country people was the fox hunt. Andrew provided a place at his farm where a fox might be kept until it was needed for a hunt.[9] For the most part the woods had no underbrush, a situation which made possible an interesting chase, at least until the fox reached the swamp. It is said that Emily once participated in these hunts on a horse named Jack, which her father had sent as a colt from Kentucky in the early fifties. But by these years of the late seventies, both she and Andrew restricted themselves to entertainments of a milder sort.[10] In the afternoon, after a full day of hunting, the guests of the Smyths changed into their best clothes, ate a large country dinner, and danced to the music of a fiddle and the piano.

Because Jasper County people had read magazines and gone to towns like Galveston more than before, manners were more formal perhaps than they had once been. The setting, however, remained as plain, if not more so, considering the wear and tear that time had made on the house. Guests usually stayed all night. The men occupied the boys' room, and the ladies used the other two bedrooms. When there were not enough beds and trundle beds to accommodate the guests, pallets made from quilts were spread on the floor or, in the warm months, some of the men slept under the trees in hammocks or on the ground. The next morning, early, the guests had breakfast and were on their way, for they, like the Smyths, had work to do at home.[11]

Early in 1879 Elias Seale moved to Beaumont, where he entered into several business enterprises. Since Beaumont was one of the *Laura's* main stopping places, Elias, besides his other ventures, could see to his partners' interests there. Some good stores had opened in Beaumont and the *Laura* always had orders to fill on the coast for Beaumont people. With Colonel Renfro still in Sabine Pass from time to time and Elias in Beaumont permanently, arrangements for freight on the *Laura* could be

---

[9] Andrew F. Smyth account book, 1852. AFS MSS.

[10] M. Constantine Smyth, Moulton, Alabama, to Andrew and Emily Smyth, June 12, 1874. AFS MSS.

[11] Mrs. George C. O'Brien to the author in a conversation, July 10, 1962.

made before the boat docked, thus avoiding unnecessary delay at the two important ports. By 1879 the operations of the *Laura* had become so efficient that the trip from the coast to Bevilport often took just seventeen days.[12]

In June, 1879, Emily and one of the grandchildren traveled with Andrew to Sabine Pass aboard the *Laura* and on to Galveston, probably using the beach coach. George and Buddy were managing the Bevilport store and the Negroes knew the routine of the farm. On the way upriver the Smyths stopped at Beaumont for two days and stayed with Elias and his family. From there they made a three-day excursion to the town of Sour Lake, about twenty-five miles outside of Beaumont. The town was named for its famous Sour Lake, whose special kind of mud was believed to be healthful. A photograph taken on this trip substantiates Emily's concern that Andrew had aged terribly and was working too hard. Renting a room in Mr. Merchant's big hotel, Andrew, Emily, and the grandchild bathed in the lake and enjoyed the company of other vacationers.[13] It was the first real vacation that they had taken since the visits to Alabama and Kentucky that summer thirty years earlier.

The owners of the *Laura* prepared for their fall business. In August and September one trip was made to the coast and, as evidenced by the order forms, it seems that affairs had never been in a more profitable condition.

On the upriver trip in October the *Laura* docked in Beaumont to deposit goods and undergo minor repairs. In the hot afternoon deckhands and workmen toyed with a broken mechanism on the lower deck. They could not mend it. Andrew, realizing what was wrong and quite irritated with the men, went to the group to describe the mending process. In the long run, of course, he did the repair work himself. Taken with a sudden headache, Andrew went to a coil of rope and lay down. A deckhand ran to get Elias, explaining that he had never seen the Captain lie down in view of his employees.

Elias hitched a surrey and went to the waterfront, where Andrew was found unconscious. In a bedroom at the Seale house a doctor pronounced the condition serious and Emily was notified at once.

As no steamboat was at Bevilport when the news reached Emily, she ordered horses and saddled for herself and Ann-Tobe. They arrived in

---

[12] Andrew F. Smyth account book for 1878–1879. AFS MSS.
[13] *Ibid.*

Beaumont days later, in the afternoon of October 22, and Andrew died during the night.

Andrew, like George, was not buried in Jasper County. George W. Smyth, Jr., offered a place beside his two children in Magnolia Cemetery on Brake's Bayou, not far from Beaumont, and hardly a stone's throw from the Neches River. It was Emily's wish that Andrew be buried there. Emily remained in Beaumont for several days making necessary arrangements with her husband's business associates. When the *Laura* headed upriver, she was aboard, concerned that she was needed at home. There were things to do before cool weather came.

BIBLIOGRAPHY

Primary Sources

I. *Manuscripts*

Bridges, Mrs. W. H.   Microfilm collection of muster rolls of the Jasper Volunteers in the Texas Revolution, the Mexican War, and the Civil War. Roganville, Texas.

Hadnot, Mollie, MS.   Consists of 8 pages dictated by Mollie Hadnot, who was born a slave in Beaumont in 1847, telling briefly her story. The pages, written in 1935, speak of Andrew Smyth's sawmill, hence, their interest here. Estate of William Seale, Beaumont, Texas.

Marshall, Eugene, MSS.   Diary and papers dealing with Galveston, Texas, 1859–1860.   Duke University Library, Durham, North Carolina.

Mellon, Sam W., MS.   A diary of a trip from Jasper in 1853 through East Texas, comparing many towns to Jasper. Rosenberg Library, Galveston, Texas.

Seale, Elisha DeKalb, MSS.   Letters and farm notes from Jasper and Tyler Counties in Texas. The some 500 items cover the years 1850–1911, but only those for the period through 1880 were used here. The collection presents an interesting, though incomplete, account of the life of a farmer and schoolteacher of the period after the Civil War. Estate of William Seale, Beaumont, Texas.

Smyth, Andrew Farney, MSS (AFS MSS).   The manuscripts from the steamer trunk, which provide the bulk of the information used in this book. Letters, account books, brief diaries, business papers, maps, field notes, order forms, a few broadsides, and other printed matter are in the collection, which spans the years 1835–1879. To this are attached the papers of Emily Allen Smyth from 1879–1907; Mrs. Smyth's papers fill in some of the voids in those of her husband. There are about 3,500 items in the steamer-trunk collection and most of them were used in one way or another in this book. Estate of William Seale, Beaumont, Texas.

Smyth, Andrew Farney, MSS (AFS MSS, Childers).   One account book of about 150 pages and 30 loose pages dealing with various business activities, 1850–1870. Collection of J. M. Childers, Jasper, Texas.

Smyth, George W., MSS (GWS MSS, TSA).   Consists of 50 items, of which most were used here. This collection is concerned with the major parts of his life. Texas State Archives, Austin, Texas.

Smyth, George W., MSS (GWS MSS, UTA). A collection of an estimated 4,000 items dealing with every phase of his life from the early 1830's to some of the transactions of his widow. Mainly the material of a personal nature was used for this book. University of Texas Archives, Austin, Texas.

Stuart, Ben, MS. Contains a useful account of the steamers on the rivers and at Galveston. Speaks at some length on cotton and the other upcountry crops. Divided under topics. Rosenberg Library, Galveston, Texas.

West, Frank J., MSS. Letters to Georgia from Texas telling the experiences of a settler of the 1850's. Duke University Library, Durham, North Carolina.

Yoakum, Henderson MS. Diary of life in Huntsville, Texas, in 1852. Yoakum Collection, University of Texas Archives, Austin, Texas.

II. *Published Diaries, Travel Books, Memoirs*

Allen, Winnie (ed.). "The Autobiography of George W. Smyth," *Southwestern Historical Quarterly,* XXXVI (January 1933), 200–214.

Almonte, Juan N. "Statistical Report on Texas (1835)," *Southwestern Historical Quarterly,* XXVIII (January 1925), 206.

Armstrong, George W. *The Memoirs of George W. Armstrong.* Edited by George Van Horn Moseley. Austin: The Steck Co., 1958. Privately Printed.

Barnard, J. H. *Dr. J. H. Barnard's Journal: December 1835–June 1836.* Edited by Hobart Huson. Goliad: Goliad Bicentennial Edition, 1950.

Bracht, Viktor. *Texas in 1848.* Translated by Charles Frank Schmidt. San Antonio: Naylor Printing Company, 1931.

DeCordova, Jr. *Texas: Her Resources and Her Public Men.* Philadelphia: J. B. Lippincott & Company, 1857.

Dresel, Gustav. *Gustav Dresel's Houston Journal: Adventures in North America and Texas, 1837–1841.* Edited and translated by Max Freund. Austin: University of Texas Press, 1954.

Freund, Max, (ed. and trans.). *Gustav Dresel's Houston Journal: Adventures in North America and Texas, 1837–1841.* Austin: University of Texas Press, 1954.

Helm, Mary S. *Scraps of Early Texas History.* Austin: B. R. Warner and Company, 1884.

Holley, Mary Austin. *Texas.* Lexington, Kentucky: J. Clarke & Company, 1836.

Hollon, Eugene, and Ruth Lapham Butler (eds.). *William Bollaert's Texas.* Norman: University of Oklahoma Press, 1956.

Huson, Hobart (ed.). *Dr. J. H. Barnard's Journal: December 1835–June 1836.* Goliad: Goliad Bicentennial Edition, 1950.

Moseley, George Van Horn (ed.). *The Memoirs of George W. Armstrong.* Austin: The Steck Company, 1958. Privately printed.

Muir, Andrew Forest (ed.). *Texas in 1837: An Anonymous Contemporary Narrative.* Austin: University of Texas Press, 1958.

Olmsted, Frederick Law. *A Journey through Texas*. New York: Dix, Edwards and Company, 1857.

Pratt, Willis W. (ed.). *Galveston Island; or a Few Months off the Coast of Texas: The Journal of Francis C. Sheridan, 1839–1840*. Austin: University of Texas Press, 1954.

Rankin, Melinda. *Texas in 1850*. Boston: Damrell & Moore, 1850.

Richardson and Company. *The Texas Almanac for 1858*. Galveston: Richardson and Company, 1857.

Roemer, Ferdinand. *Texas*. Translated by Oswald Mueller. San Antonio: Standard Printing Company, 1935.

Sheridan, Francis. *Galveston Island, or a Few Months off the Coast of Texas: The Journal of Francis C. Sheridan, 1839–1840*. Edited by Willis Pratt. Austin: University of Texas Press, 1954.

Smither, Harriet (ed.). "Diary of Adolphus Sterne," *Southwestern Historical Quarterly*, XXXVI (January 1933), 215–230.

Smithwick, Noah. *The Evolution of a State*. Austin: The Steck Company, 1935.

Smyth, George W. "The Autobiography of George W. Smyth," Edited by Winnie Allen, *Southwestern Historical Quarterly*, XXXVI (January 1933), 200–214.

Sterne, Adolphus. "Diary of Adolphus Sterne." Edited by Harriet Smither, *Southwestern Historical Quarterly*, XXXVI (January 1933), 215–230.

Stiff, Edward. *The Texas Emigrant*. Cincinnati: George Conclin, 1840.

Suthron, A. (alias). *Prairiedom: Rambles and Scrambles in Texas or New Estremadura*. New York: Paine & Burgess, 1845.

Texas in 1837: An Anonymous Contemporary Narrative. Austin: University of Texas Press, 1958.

Woodman, David, Jr. *Guide to Texas Emigrants*. Boston: M. Hawes, 1835.

III. *Interviews and Other Sources*

I have had the advantage of knowing several of the grandchildren and great grandchildren of Andrew Smyth, and while none of them remember the Captain himself most of them knew Mrs. Smyth when they were children. The various interviews which appear in the footnotes have been a valuable addition to the material in the manuscripts. The information I attribute to interviews is not heresay. Those stories I have used were suggested in some way in the manuscripts before being employed in the book; having these recollections from relatives has been an asset, for they fill in with anecdotes those brief, bare periods which might be left if I did not go beyond the letters and other papers.

A surprising number of the Smyths' personal belongings remain scattered, both within and outside the Smyth family. I have been able to locate many of these belongings and through the account books have actually been able to substantiate when they appeared in the Smyths' lives. One will find mention of these various items scattered through the book.

SECONDARY SOURCES

Barns, Florence Elberta. *A Texas Calendar.* Dallas: Tardy Publishing Company, 1935.

Beaumont Journal, The. Beaumont, Texas.

Binkley, William C. *The Texas Revolution.* Baton Rouge: Louisiana State University Press, 1952.

Boone, William. "The Anglo-American Migration to East Texas." Unpublished MA thesis, Duke University, 1941.

Carroll, H. Bailey. "Texas Collection," *Southwestern Historical Quarterly,* L (July 1946), 117.

Carroll, J. M. *A History of Texas Baptists.* Dallas: Baptist Standard Publishing Company, 1923.

Duval, J. C. *Early Times in Texas.* Austin: H. P. N. Gammell & Co., 1892.

East Texas Clarion, The. Jasper, Texas.

Elliott, Claude. "Alabama and the Texas Revolution," *Southwestern Historical Quarterly,* L (January 1947), 315–328.

Fornell, Earl Wesley. *The Galveston Era: The Texas Crescent on the Eve of Secession.* Austin: University of Texas Press, 1961.

Hardy, Dermot H. and Ingham S. Roberts (eds.). *Historical Review of South-East Texas.* Chicago: The Lewis Publishing Company, 1910.

Hartley, Oliver C. *A Digest of Texas Laws.* Philadelphia: Thomas Cowperthwait & Co., 1850.

Hogan, William Ransom. *The Texas Republic: A Social and Economic History.* Norman: University of Oklahoma Press, 1946.

James, Marquis. *The Raven: A Biography of Sam Houston.* New York: Blue Ribbon Books, Inc., 1929.

Jasper Newsboy, The. Jasper, Texas.

Jones, Katharine M. *The Plantation South.* New York: The Bobbs-Merrill Company, Inc., 1957.

Journal of the Texas Convention of 1866. Austin: State of Texas, 1866.

Kemp, L. W. *The Signers of the Texas Declaration of Independence.* Houston: The Anson Jones Press, 1944.

Lathrop, Barnes F. *Migration into East Texas 1835–1860.* Austin: The Texas State Historical Association, 1949.

Myers, Elbert Jefferson. "Life of George W. Smyth." Unpublished MA thesis at The University of Texas, 1931.

Norvell, Mrs. Lipscomb. *King's Highway.* San Antonio: The National Old Trails Road in Texas, 1945.

Owsley, Frank Lawrence. *Plain Folk of the Old South.* Baton Rouge: Louisiana State University Press, 1949.

Parmer, William Tellis. *Seventy-Five Years in Nacogdoches: A History of the First Baptist Church.* Dallas: The Dorsey Company, 1959.

Saunders, James Edmund. *Early Settlers of Alabama.* New Orleans: L. Graham and Son, Ltd., 1899.

Schmitz, Joseph William. *Texas Culture in the Days of the Republic.* San Antonio: The Naylor Company, 1960.

Shanklin, Felda Davis. *Early Days in Texas.* San Antonio: The Naylor Company, 1953.

Siegel, Stanley. *A Political History of the Texas Republic, 1836–1845.* Austin: University of Texas Press, 1956.

Sloan, Eric. *America Yesterday.* New York: Wilfred Funk, Inc., 1956.

Smith, J. Frazier. *White Pillars: Early Life and Architecture of the Lower Mississippi Valley Country.* New York: William Helburn, Inc., 1941.

Stratton, Florence. *The Story of Beaumont.* n. d., n. p., circa 1925.

Sunday Enterprise, The. Beaumont, Texas.

Webb, Walter Prescott *et al. Handbook of Texas.* Austin: Texas State Historical Association, 1952.

Weekly Civilian & Gazette, Galveston, Texas.

Wortham, Louis J. *A History of Texas from Wilderness to Commonwealth.* Vols. 3, 4, 5. Fort Worth: Wortham-Molyneaux Company, 1924.

Yoakum, Henderson. *History of Texas from Its First Settlement in 1685 to Its Annexation to the United States in 1846.* Vol. II. New York: J. S. Redfield, 1855.

INDEX

*In this Index, Andrew, Emily, George, and Frances Smyth
are referred to by first name only.*